CHAOS
IN OUR
COLLEGES

CHAOS
IN OUR
COLLEGES

by Morris Freedman

Department of English
University of New Mexico

DAVID McKAY COMPANY, INC.

New York

CHAOS IN OUR COLLEGES

To Jacques Barzun

PREFACE

THIS is a personal view of the American academic landscape. I stand on no other man's promontory; indeed, I stand on no promontory very long. My vision of that landscape combines perspectives from various high spots, from valleys, from out-of-the-way corners, from familiar meadows. But while I have always been personal, I have always tried to see the landscape as in itself it really is, to adapt Arnold. I have lived long in the academic countryside, I live in it now, and when I have left it for brief periods, I have come back, I think, with new perspectives. Memory here is mingled with impression, observation, analysis, speculation, and projection; I claim accuracy only for what is personal, within the usual limits of distortion that the personal filter will always work; I claim at least fairness and an attempt at judiciousness for the rest.

My sense of the scene is based on a geographic range as well as on a range of experience. I have, of course, been an undergraduate and a graduate student; I have taught at a large urban university in the East and am teaching at a middle-sized one in the Southwest; I have visited, to teach or to study, universities and libraries on both coasts. I have briefly administered several academic enterprises. I have talked with colleagues in the West, smog in my eyes, and with those in the East; I have visited large, small, and middle-sized institutions across the country, experimental and conventional. I have poked around such non-university academic enclaves as research libraries, magazines, and government offices. My share of scholarship and criticism has appeared in the proper journals. I have attended national conventions as job-hunter, paper-reader, and job-interviewer.

Which all adds up not to any conclusion that I feel myself an "authority" on the subject, but to the conclusion that I am an authority on very little indeed, perhaps only on what goes on in my own classroom and on my own desk. The academic country is certainly my country, but there is no one so blind about his surroundings as a long-time resident anywhere. I don't wish to justify myself when I point out that anthropologists from the mainland sometimes understand a distant island culture better than their own. I do say that it has been valuable for me to look around at my world, and that I have become more conscious of all of the landscape in doing so. I see this world from the inside, from the inside as a citizen and a worker in it. I see it through my own senses, values, instincts, personality. I claim no definitiveness for my report, only some degree of individuality, and in this may lie any value it has.

Of course, I have incurred many debts, not just to the persons I have talked and argued with, and occasionally listened to, but also to the writers of the many published and unpublished documents I have read. I thank them all warmly and humbly, but I shall not embarrass anyone by listing names, for I have turned so much to personal use, a use often quite out of harmony with original intentions.

There have not been enough studies of the academic landscape that fall between the improvisation of fiction and the controlled scrutiny of the sociological project. An essayistic study like mine surely has its own limitations, but these are not the same as those of fiction or sociology. The essay, too, reveals the world.

MORRIS FREEDMAN

ALBUQUERQUE, NEW MEXICO
JUNE, 1963

CONTENTS

CHAOS
IN OUR
COLLEGES

CHAOS
IN OUR
COLLEGES

AMERICAN higher education is involved, like a number of other national enterprises, in a thorough and frequently agonizing appraisal. Just about everyone is looking at the academic scene. We have statisticians and historians, concerned with facts and figures, and journalists and sociologists, concerned with the peculiarities and problems of the present and the trends for the future. We have a group of new specialists, the academic sociologists and the foundation experts. Hardly an issue of a weekly book review fails to carry a notice or a review of a new study having to do with the academic world. Publications have sprung up, focusing on the subject. One publisher issues a house letter, "What the Colleges Are Doing," since, obviously, they are doing all sorts of things these days no one would have imagined them doing just a decade ago. Foundations issue brochures and leaflets, some of them dealing with specialized problems, like "superior" students. We even have a *Journal of Higher Education*. General journals like *Harper's*, *The Atlantic*, *The Saturday Review*, *The Reporter*, devote whole issues to higher education. We have a new literary genre, the academic novel, which offers a perspective generally not to be found in objective studies, whose forthrightness may be limited by the method of research or merely by the laws of libel.

The landscape of higher education is indeed intriguing today. Wherever one looks, one may see something new or something odd or something changing right before one's eyes. Some schools are still back in the 'twenties, with football and flappers dominating their images; some still teach and actually require students to take Latin; some offer degrees to beauty parlor operators or playground specialists. Schools are being forced to redefine, sometimes just to define for the first time, their character and aims. Some cannot take the time or provide the thought for definition; they just metamorphose into something else. The pressures to change (or remain the same, as in the Deep South) are enormous, and very few institutions can resist or control them, let alone use them productively; many easily and lazily become unbalanced or distorted.

The most insistent pressure has the force of nature itself: the increased number of young men and women of college age in the population. And this pressure is intensified by the wish of more and more young people every year to get a college education. But there are strong pressures, too, from government, industry, and the foundations, exerted in various ways, to emphasize certain areas, to teach in certain ways, to produce certain results, sometimes, even, to show "a profit." Our entire society has come to expect something of our universities. Legislators, admirals, newspaper editors all issue announcements of what universities should and must do, from winning more football games, to holding classes 365 days a year, to firing professors who don't exalt the glories of American capitalism.

Civilized universities, with the aid and understanding of civilized members of the public, have more or less learned to cope with many of the more maniacal external pressures.

2

The invisible, sometimes scarcely perceptible, internal pressures are more difficult to deal with. But they affect the body academic no less severely, and, like any such pressures, sometimes more severely because they are invisible and often insidious. These have to do with the interior terrain. A graduate school may come to dominate a university. A particular college may want, in effect, to adulterate a college degree because some of its students cannot, or will not, take or pass certain courses. The engineering and science departments will seek to monopolize their students' time. A university will systematically raid others for faculty talent (a practice given precedent and respectability by the long-time raiding for athletic stars). Under the sacred rallying cry of academic freedom, mediocre faculties seek to dominate administrations. Or, conversely, under the almost equally sacred slogan of efficiency and responsibility, administrations will be willful and tyrannical.

Perhaps more than ever before in our history, it seems important to establish the status of an institution. Applicants and their parents are anxious to get the most for their investment. New doctors of philosophy, considering a first appointment or an offer that means rising in rank and pay, develop an uncanny instinct for considering the prestige of institutions. Foundations, like good investors anywhere (and foundations have all been created through the fruits of good investment), want to put their money on the surest thing. There are blue chip colleges just as there are blue chip corporations; there are good if unspectacular stocks and there are even unlisted ones—to complete the metaphor.

What makes a college or university good? The quality of its teaching? The students? Its size? The amount of research and scholarship produced? Its library? How its graduates make out? How many Ph.D.'s on the faculty? All of these are considered, of course. A few minutes in a library

3

will give us clear-cut information about any of the above questions except the first. Someone, someplace, will have recorded how many full-time students every college or university has registered; how many books its library boasts of; how many of its graduates go into graduate school or into business, and how they have performed on the Graduate Record Examination; how large an endowment it has; what are the lowest and highest and average salaries of every professorial rank; etc., etc.

But the standing of a university, it seems universally agreed, depends finally on the quality of its teaching, especially if we conceive of research and scholarship as components of teaching. This measure is accepted both inside and outside the universities. Now, unless we simply count the number of Nobel Prize winners on a faculty (many of whom have probably been relieved of all teaching assignments anyway), or the number of professors who have taken jobs with the federal government, we can use only indirect estimates of quality of teaching.

Certainly the most widely applied criterion is the number of publications, usually books, the faculty has produced. Aside from what effect the standard of publication may have had on the character of teaching, it has produced a glorious scramble among schools to get "productive" professors. Administrators actively lure away from other institutions anyone who publishes a good deal or gives promise of so doing. Where once football heroes or coaches used to bring fame and fortune to alma mater, by getting their names and pictures into sports pages throughout the country, now professors bring this fame, by getting their books or articles published, sometimes even with their pictures, listing their academic affiliation. A good argument may be made out for using publication as a measure of teaching quality, no doubt, but it has become almost pernicious to

4

concentrate so exclusively on this particular measure. Certainly publication does not answer the question of how good the teaching is for a high school graduate wondering whether to go to a particular place. Indeed, an enormous publication fame may well in some instances be considered a sign that a faculty is more concerned with getting into print than with teaching students.

Several state universities, driven possibly by the same civic pride that impels the state's businessmen to boast of having the largest transient population or the largest navel orange crop or the largest number of Miss Americas, have tried to build departments with the largest number of prolific professors in the country. Private schools try to fulfill the same ambition. Some have built specialized libraries unparalleled in the world; the largest collection on sex in the world is at the Kinsey Institute at Indiana University. Probably the best collection of material on James Joyce is at the University of Buffalo. Obviously much of this eagerness to be first, largest, and best has produced much that is worthy, for the school, for the state, and for the nation. But, occasionally, the relentless, ceaseless searching for academic uniqueness and distinction has left poorer areas of the country barren or inadequately provided for.

The drive toward greatness or, at least, uniqueness produces more problems, certainly, than successes. Woodrow Wilson Fellows, graduate students preparing for teaching careers in college, will funnel into a handful of the "best" places, one or two universities on the West Coast, one or two in the Mid-west, three or four on the East Coast. There, lost among crowds of other graduate students similarly lured, they lose their eagerness and drive, and they drift away into other fields. The whole point of their fellowship is thus negated. Young faculty members, looking for their first appointment, will aim single-mindedly at one of the prestige institutions, ready to sacrifice decent salary, decent teaching assignment, decent living conditions, anything to live and work in the aura of fame and importance. Even undergraduates, blinded by the dazzle of the brilliant graduate faculty, will submit themselves to mass-production, assembly-line teaching.

Institutions themselves lose their sense of identity, of proportion and pride. "We like to think of ourselves as a small Berkeley," I heard one faculty member say of his small state institution. Throughout the country, in private as well as in public colleges, faculty and administration take their cue all too often from Berkeley or from Harvard. No doubt many cues should be taken from these estimable schools, and if every college and university could reasonably hope to become a Berkeley or a Harvard, we might possibly have something like academic paradise (at least for some). But cues should not be taken from elsewhere when they are not appropriate or realistic, or when other and occasionally better cues may be at hand.

It should be time to acknowledge that not very many universities can hope to equal in every field the academic level of Berkeley, Harvard, Columbia, Yale, or Princeton, however we define that level. We simply do not have enough Nobel Prize winners to go around, for one thing, or enough distinguished faculty generally, or, simply, enough money. And there are not enough students in the country to profit from a dozen or so Berkeleys and Harvards. Nor should universities want simply to equal those schools. For all of their virtues, they have not yet worked out a way for including all of the academic delights. A Harvard cannot be an Antioch, nor a Berkeley a University of New Mexico. Smallness has its own characteristic virtues.

In addition to exploiting their own possibilities for virtues, other institutions than those on Olympus might well

6

want to emphasize a particular area or discipline or approach. Harvard is not doing what St. Johns or Antioch does. The University of New Mexico has a rich, solid program in Latin American Studies, not quite equaled elsewhere. Its honors program offers good students some of the advantages of the small Mid-western and Eastern colleges. Its anthropology department is among the best in the country. Colleges in the South might well examine the problems of their region as those in other sections have studied their problems. In the shadow of the California colossi, the small Associated Colleges at Claremont offer individual and specialized attention to graduates and undergraduates in a setting which does not neglect the more private amenities. A journey from the UCLA campus to Claremont is like a trip from Times Square to the square of a charming New England village. It is not essential for every university to have a cyclotron, or a library that is unparalleled in the world. The difference for a university—for its students particularly —between a Nobelist in physics and a first-rate physicist who can teach and carry out research is really not great. State aggie universities might frequently concentrate on merely improving their liberal arts colleges than on trying to offer Ph.D.'s in every area that Berkeley does.

As more and more colleges focus their best energies on efforts to rise to some remote and often irrelevant standard of superiority (not excellence necessarily), they often neglect the problems at hand. Some of these are common, of course, to all institutions at the moment. The large and great schools as well as the small and modest ones have to deal with the huge numbers of high school graduates demanding admission. Where do we get the qualified teachers for them? Must we continue to insist on the Ph.D. for every college professor? Can we increase class size or go to television without adulterating what we hope to give them?

Can some students learn without classes altogether? How do we separate the superior students from the hordes, and how do we take care of their special needs? How much is needed in scholarship aid, where should the money come from, and how should the aid be distributed? How much emphasis should be given to liberal subjects as opposed to professional ones? Just how might we determine who are the good teachers and who the poor ones—other than by counting number of words published per month?

And there are local problems which must not be neglected lest they ultimately produce an effect on the academic world at large. How much power should mediocre faculties be allowed to exercise to protect themselves? Should colleges of education be allowed to administer or in any way guide junior colleges? Should they concern themselves at all with the question of college teaching?

None of these questions is neglected in the growing body of studies of higher education. Indeed, some of them are being answered many times over, and some are still being posed as though they had never come up before. It is probably of some value to have affirmed over and over that, in many situations, no teaching machine, no television set, no combination of mechanical and audio-visual aids of any sort can replace the competent, living, responding, imaginatively functioning professor in the classroom. We now have a number of studies and speculations suggesting that good students might profit from more independent study. We know as conclusively as we know anything that good college teachers will be in short supply in the very near future. And it is often healthy and necessary to be told some of these things several times in different ways: the cumbersome academic plant works wondrously slow to change itself.

But the repetition of studies already done, the asking of questions already asked, the concentration on one or two problems to the exclusion or slighting of other equally important ones, testify to inefficiency and lack of orientation. The competition which marks American business operation, with all its inevitable secrecy about profits and changes in merchandise, too often sets the pattern for academic competition. Not only do schools openly compete for the ready money for fashionable projects, but even the foundations and the government, in its very small way, compete with each other to offer the money, to set themselves up first in a particular area. Students become confused about what careers to prepare for and how best to do so. The academic world subjects them to the same battery of conflicting claims as do the automobile and cigarette manufacturers. Shall they become scientists, engineers, college teachers, physicians, government administrators? Faculty members, too, find themselves caught up in the near chaos, defending curricula in pure science or technology, over-insisting on the humanities, urging new areas for study altogether. In short, American higher education does not know where it is going, does not even know where it wants to go, all the while it is proposing new ways of getting somewhere. An official in the United States Office of Education conceded to me that determining the direction and destination of American higher education should be a priority duty of the office, but that it lacks funds, personnel, and authority. Meanwhile, only the loudest voice, the largest grant, the most energetic and ambitious administrator, determine our objectives from moment to moment, from grant to grant.

It is meaningless, even dangerous perhaps, to insist that one of our goals must be to produce as many engineers and scientists each year as does Russia. College graduates should never be counted like units off an assembly line. If we do count them this way, we may find ourselves suddenly overproducing, with a surplus in one area, a shortage in another. We should no more let Russia determine our goals in education than we let her set our goals in politics, business, or living conditions. This does not mean that we should ever close our eyes to realities; it does mean that we should not let ourselves be hypnotized or blinded by one reality to the exclusion of other, no less compelling realities. Nor should we let ourselves succumb to the blandishments of our internal equalizers, who insist that every American is entitled to a college degree, even if this means changing the traditional substance of a college education. We must be constantly sensitive to special demands, narrow needs, isolated requirements. Americans have learned to sell just about anything through the powers of persuasion, and they have also learned to buy just about anything. While it may make little difference to respond to advertising in the world at large, and may sometimes even do good, it seems to me desperately urgent not to be quick and easy in responding to special pleas in the turbulent world of higher education.

The landscape is busy. We must look at it panoramically, from some detached perspective. Too many of us are caught up in one part or another of the territory, oblivious of the whole. Not that detachment will surely provide some magical system for ordering the confusion. The confusion, the competition, the duplication and overlapping of effort, may all be necessary, preliminary, to growth. We may well decide that many of the problems are unique, not connected with anything else, and should remain isolated. But we should come to any such decisions from a large perspective, not from a parochial lack of it.

Now that we are so openly and systematically examining the nature of American higher education, we should do so with unlimited honesty. We must look far as well as near. Both the heights and the plains, the future and the immediate, must concern us. Facts are always fine, but we must use them to form opinions, in the interest of values—values which in the largest sense we are all agreed upon: to keep America, and Western civilization itself, free, by making man fully informed, fully aware of his human potential, and by making him able to fulfill it.

LET'S
REDISTRIBUTE
OUR ACADEMIC
WEALTH

YEAR BY YEAR, academic wealth and power in the United States—the best professors, the best students, the rarest books, the largest and latest cyclotrons, the most elaborate laboratories, the biggest grants, the most handsome bequests—have been going to fewer and fewer campuses. It may be in the highest interests of efficiency and economy for automobile manufacturing in the country to reduce itself to four or five companies, with two of them unquestionably leading the field. But it is neither efficient nor economical, not healthy or wise, for a similar concentration to take place in higher education.

The distribution (up to May 1961) of the 46 American Nobel Prize winners connected with universities and colleges offers a dramatic illustration of this concentration: they were to be found in a total of 17 institutions. Heading the list were Harvard and the University of California, with 8 each; Columbia had 6; Cal Tech, 5; Stanford and Washington University, 3 each; the University of Chicago and Cornell, 2 each; and Indiana, Carnegie Tech, Rutgers, NYU, Wisconsin, St. Louis, Illinois, Rochester, and Western Reserve, 1 each.

Nobel Prizes, of course, are not awarded in every discipline. If we look for America's most distinguished historians, sociologists, economists, political scientists, psychologists, philosophers, literary scholars, biologists, archaeologists, geologists, mathematicians, we will find them distributed among an equally small number of colleges, with the University of California and Harvard again probably leading the list. We can fairly estimate that perhaps 25 of this country's institutions of higher learning harbor our leading scientists, social scientists, and humanists, that is, of those persons still in academic life.

This is a striking imbalance. About a thousand institutions offer baccalaureate, master's, and doctor's degrees in this country. Even if we exclude all strictly denominational schools, professional colleges, teachers' colleges, specialized schools of various sorts, and all others dubiously entitled to be described as institutions of higher learning, we still have about forty to fifty respectable state and city colleges and universities and perhaps three to four times that number of respectable private ones. In short, about one tenth of the nation's schools of higher learning have creamed off about 90 per cent of the nation's professorial wealth.

The cornering of the market in distinguished professors has become one of the primary functions of college administrations with appropriate resources. In California, administrators congratulate themselves publicly on having the foresight to pick potential Nobelists for their faculties. Purdue University recently collected more than twenty of the country's top mathematicians in one large-scale operation. Department chairmen and deans in quite decent but poor schools spend much of their time, energy, and money trying to help their better faculty resist the blandishments of wealthier institutions.

We cannot, then, attribute the gathering in of famous professors by so few campuses merely to the normal operation of the academic market. At one time, perhaps, the

13

advantages of certain library holdings, of certain physical facilities, of geography and climate, of the presence of distinguished colleagues in associated fields, might have all operated to attract personages. Today, however, administrators single-mindedly set out to get academic celebrities, sometimes with little to offer except handsome salaries and luxurious working conditions (like no students and no office hours). Southern Illinois University, for instance, in Carbondale, a little mining town in the southern part of the state, has in a very short time leaped into national prominence with several well-known faculty members. The University of California in Riverside is another school that has, nearly overnight, collected a number of distinguished professors.

The trend obviously has much to justify it. Given a need for a good college in a particular area, as well as the money and the intelligence to meet this need, the quickest way for a school to build itself some sort of national reputation is to hire men of distinction. (Intelligence as well as taste, wisdom, and experience are necessary to distinguish between mere paper fame and genuine worth, and sometimes the distinction is not made so long as the professor comes trailing with him some aura of reputation.) And it is perfectly natural for established schools with substantial endowments—like Harvard, Yale, or Columbia—or for state institutions well-favored of rich legislatures—like those in California, Indiana, and Illinois—to keep spending their considerable funds in the traditional ways of universities: hiring new faculty, increasing salaries, building library holdings, establishing presses, expanding plant, sponsoring research and scholarship. It is natural for wealth to attract wealth. A young and suddenly renowned professor will likely find a California or Harvard offer of appointment more tempting than one from a conservative Mid-western university, even if all other things are equal. And it is natural for the government to award a contract, or a foundation a grant, to an institution that has the finest facilities and personnel.

But the trend, if natural, is hardly good. The competition among the Big Twenty-five suggests the dangers. It has certainly been in every way healthy that faculty salaries have gone up generally as the California giants have bid against the Eastern ones. Teaching and research conditions have also improved somewhat as a result; at the very least, schools hoping to remain in the competition have recognized the need for improving them. But in the large perspective the disadvantages outweigh any benefits, which are indirect anyway. (We should have the benefits without the disadvantageous side effects.)

Very often, for example, when an institution succeeds in outbidding a rival, it gains a celebrity while the academic world loses a teacher. One of the common lures is the promise of little or no teaching. Yale was able not long ago to get a distinguished Berkeley professor for a year's visit by offering, in addition to a salary in the twenty-thousand-dollar bracket, secretarial help, travel funds, and absolutely no classroom assignments.

Certainly scholars and teachers can use profitably an occasional year free of classroom chores; the sabbatical in fact insures that they get it in one form or another. But too often the offer to release a celebrity from any teaching is not prompted by good academic reasons. Most of the time an institution merely wants to have its name associated with an active, respectable scholar or scientist. Such an association will attract lesser known but promising faculty, better students, and larger and larger grants and donations. More and more, institutions hire well known persons neither to teach nor to read nor to meet students nor to do research, but simply to lend their names in order to attract more money. Celebrities are expected to have connections in Washington or on the boards of foundations. Not many professors, even Olympian ones, can withstand the temptations made in such flattering and sumptuary terms.

Now, it is academically of the first importance for faculty and students, graduate and undergraduate, to have a personage in their midst, whether he's a Nobelist in literature or a philosopher, and whether or not he teaches. William Faulkner was left pretty much to his own devices at the University of Virginia, and so was Robert Frost when he was in residence at Amherst and elsewhere. All academic great men make contributions to our store of wisdom, which is a universal treasure, and there is no more natural place for them to live and work than on a campus. But in a more immediate sense, it is essential to learning in colleges and universities for students to be in the physical presence, from time to time, of persons who have become names, whose books and articles and research are the substance of contemporary knowledge, who work on the frontiers of the arts and sciences. It is valuable for everyone on a campus to encounter the great, to ask questions of them, to argue with them, to see that greatness has its roots in familiar mortality. Encounters with the great extend our own sense of reach, and sometimes even our grasp.

But if such encounters are essential to the Harvard or to the Berkeley communities, they are no less essential to colleges and universities in Kansas, Nebraska, Arizona, Utah, Wyoming, and New Mexico. Eight Nobelists on a campus do not do more for it in this regard than, say, four.

More importantly, too, a redistribution of our academic forces would help tremendously to raise the level of whole disciplines. Twenty leading mathematicians will not necessarily accomplish more in one school than, sensibly distributed, in five. In five schools, they would likely raise the level of work, of teaching and of research, of five departments. A vigorous, imaginative, productive, alert historian or literary scholar would hardly affect any more the quality of departments at Berkeley, Harvard, or Yale, but he might certainly stimulate colleagues and students in schools which do not have the aggregations of personages to be found at the Big Twenty-five.

Americans tend to overbuild. Many of the Big Twenty-five could maintain strong, first-rate departments in various disciplines, and present a total image of distinction, with only a fraction of their present personnel. Like some college football teams, they have two and three squads of equal strength. (And occasionally they may find themselves with three tackles and no ends, like schools which may have three or four experts on the New Deal but will be thin in certain other important areas in history.) It is sometimes simple extravagance to have departments in depth. What frequently happens at the Big Twenty-five is that perfectly reputable professors who have not attained quite the status of celebrity, or at least of the first magnitude of celebrity, find themselves relegated to lesser roles. The atmosphere of competition that begins to prevail when celebrities jostle each other in the halls becomes as pervasive and as irritating as smog itself.

A young assistant professor at a California university, famous for collecting writers of books, described his department's attitude toward publication as follows: "When you sign out at the end of the week, you punch on an IBM card the number of words you have published in the last seven days. The computer then begins clicking away. It scores the data objectively, by giving weights to number of footnotes, number of pages, and the publication. Certain publishers and journals, you see, get higher weights. You get your card back with scores evaluating your chances, considering the current competition, for having your contract renewed, for getting a promotion, for getting a salary raise, and for getting the office of your choice." He exaggerated the details but not the principle, and the bitterness was not just his alone.

Interdepartmental rivalry in some schools among the Big Twenty-five is keen, sometimes bitter, often farcical. One department in a Big Twenty-five school without a Nobelist and unsuccessful in enticing celebrities from Harvard, Columbia, or Yale has taken to issuing monthly bulletins listing publications and projects in progress of its members to establish its parity with more illustrious departments on the campus.

Students are perhaps the worst victims of the concentration of academic power. They flock, reasonably enough, to the campuses with our contemporary famous men, only to find that the men keep themselves hidden or, if they offer classes, that their enrollments are so huge that public address systems become necessary. In California, a creative writing seminar once registered 125 students. When I attended Columbia University after World War II, candidates for the master's degree in English were treated, almost necessarily, like students in bonehead composition. One lecture course had students sitting on the steps of the huge auditorium. The famous men themselves—badgered, harried, sought out like their counterparts in entertainment or public life—become in self-protection waspish, defensively curt, arrogantly remote.

Of course, students at the Big Twenty-five schools who manage to survive and to penetrate the barriers surrounding the celebrities will find themselves, especially in the physical sciences where one often works side by side with a professor, in the presence of truly great men. But often, to

18

survive in the graduate school of one of the Big Twenty-five, a student must bring with him the additional and perhaps irrelevant talents of a patience and perseverance approaching stubbornness and an unflagging capacity to elbow one's way through a crowd.

The fate of our graduate students in the face of the continuing concentration of academic wealth is crucial to the issue, for they will be the college teachers, the professional men, the scientists and engineers, the public administrators of the future. Various agencies are now supporting more and more of them through the years of graduate study. The best ones, like the best faculty, funnel into the Big Twenty-five schools where the drop-out rate for graduate students has always been high. Woodrow Wilson Fellows cluster in Harvard, Berkeley, Yale, Columbia, Stanford. What this means, of course, is that a higher percentage of the better graduate students is lost to the country than of the average students. (The reasons for dropping out of the Columbia graduate school, I remember, often had nothing to do with a student's merit: good ones often could not put up with the assembly-line indifference while poor ones grinned, bore it, perhaps thrived on it, and eventually got their degrees.)

Graduate faculty at the Big Twenty-five often simply cannot give the individual attention to students which graduate study requires. Aside from having to cope with the peculiar pressures of their own jobs, the professors have too many students working in their area. The numbers are staggering. One of the California giants had over 500 graduate students in English alone when I visited the campus; nearby, the graduate English department of a small institution, with no less distinguished a faculty, had only a dozen or so students. Nor can faculty at the big schools always properly carry out one of the important functions of graduate departments, the sensible placing of their grad-

19

uates in appropriate jobs. Some departments in the Big Twenty-five are known to write inflated, stereotyped letters of recommendation for all their students; as a consequence, graduates of these schools are considered most skeptically at hiring time.

The existence of the Big Twenty-five tends to distort the ambitions of future college teachers. Like undergraduate and graduate applicants, they will too commonly allow themselves to be lured by the brilliant wattage these schools emit in the total academic landscape. They will be ready to sacrifice decent working conditions, decent salary, decent climate and physical setting, all for the sake of basking in the heat of fame. The basking may well be briefly salutary and delightful, but it can scarcely take the place of a solid career. For every one college instructor who establishes himself in a Big Twenty-five school, there must be a half dozen who begin there a career of academic vagabondage, transferring from school to school, or who simply drift out into private industry, where at least some are occasionally encouraged to sink deep roots instead of shallow ones.

Fortunately the trend toward bigness and monopoly in the academic world is not irreversible. Indeed some attempts have already been made to slow it. The Carnegie Foundation, for example, provided the Universities of Hawaii and Alaska with funds to bring distinguished faculty to their campuses for periods of a year or longer. Similar enterprises may be cited on the mainland, but these are isolated and haphazard. Foundations, as they study ways of improving higher education, will surely see their way clear to endowing on a large scale visiting professorships at schools which simply could not afford to have distinguished men except for single lectures. A series of such endowed professorships, systematically assigned throughout the country where the needs are greatest, should do much to establish a more equitable distribution of our academic wealth. No school sparing a distinguished man for a year or two would be hurt; it might even be benefited, for it would sometimes do the man and the institution good for him to be attached to a lesser institution: so many of our great professors at Eastern schools only cross the ocean when they take a leave; some have never been west of the Mississippi. Ideally, the foundations might permanently endow professorships at other schools than the Big Twenty-five.

As our distinguished academicians spread out more evenly through the land, as the lesser schools all rise to a level of minimally decent quality, we can expect that good graduate students will also spread out. To encourage them, it might be well for graduate stipends to be awarded on the understanding that the fellows will not funnel into a handful of institutions. In addition, funds for graduate fellowships might be made available directly to institutions other than the Big Twenty-five, on a somewhat less specialized basis than is at present provided for under the National Defense Education Act, so that they will be enabled to compete at least financially with some of the giants. Funds might generally be assigned so that salary levels throughout the country for all faculty might be made more nearly equal, thus minimizing, again, one of the advantages the Big Twenty-five undoubtedly possess.

The U. S. Office of Education might well determine what the proper government role is to counter the worst effects of academic monopoly. Just as the government has been dubious about the growth of business trusts (under both Republican and Democratic administrations), and has established means for discouraging such growth, from instituting anti-trust suits to making loans to small business firms, it might explore the possibilities for establishing and maintaining a healthier academic balance. I do not suggest any-

21

thing like anti-monopoly action against the Big Twenty-five. We will always need an "elite" corps of schools, to set standards, to pioneer in new areas, to carry on the vast educational projects that will always be necessary. But I do think that means might properly be found to help the Small Two Hundred determine and satisfy their needs. The help might range from providing experts (as is now done to some extent for states, on the elementary and high school level) to providing funds, in the form of loans or grants, to carry into effect the results of such study. The resources of such federal agencies as the National Science Foundation might well be employed in this effort. Certainly a number of agencies in Washington study and help various areas of industry in this way; at least one small office might do the same systematically, thoroughly, and objectively for our academic society.

Let it be clear that I am not suggesting that great libraries or physics laboratories be broken up and distributed throughout the country, book by book and test-tube by test-tube. Nor am I suggesting that we try to duplicate elsewhere Harvard's library or Cal Tech's laboratories. But it might well be possible to raise the level elsewhere of the sort of research and teaching that can be done without a Widener Library and without a betatron. Theoretical physics, some areas in mathematics, philosophy, literary criticism, creative work in the arts, contemporary history—a number of disciplines and sub-disciplines do not depend inevitably on an extensive research or library plant. And with modern methods of micro-photography and the extensive system of inter-library loans, even many library facilities have become nearly universally available. For specialists who do need unusual equipment not available on their campus, funds might be made available for them to get to this equipment.

22

The operation of the Associated Colleges at Claremont, in California, suggests another way of handling the problems. There, the constituent colleges support a central library and a central auditorium and arrange for exchanges of faculty. Thus, a school which may be able to afford a distinguished scholar in one field but not in another will have the benefits of both. But the Claremont plan may not work with schools that are not geographically close to one another. Such plans are being attempted in the Great Lakes region, in the Mid-west, and in New England.

Still another way of decentralizing our academic power would be for schools to emphasize subjects and areas related to their geographic location. Experts on the oceans belong properly in schools on the Atlantic and Pacific seaboards; those on the Pueblo and Navajo Indians, in the Southwest; on mining, in mining country; on urban sociology, in large cities. At present, as a result of the grabbing up of prominent persons in every field by the Big Twenty-five, many such experts find themselves far removed from the center of their interest.

The government and the foundations might also encourage the Small Two Hundred to build departments of distinction not only in geographically appropriate areas but in new subject areas as well. It does happen that the foremost centers for the study of certain subjects have never been at the Big Twenty-five. Fordham University has long been prominent in earthquake studies; Tulane University, in pre-Columbian archeology; San Francisco State College, Iowa, and Stanford, in creative writing.

One need hardly stress the urgency today to use the nation's academic resources most effectively. But even if we did not have an immediate reason to advance efficiently and imaginatively on all scientific and technological fronts, not neglecting the humanities and social sciences, it is simply

23

wasteful not to use all of our academic wealth as sensibly as we can. Redistributing our academic riches can hurt no one in the long run, not even those giants which have by the force of circumstances been gorging themselves into elephantine proportions, and it can help everyone. We can even imagine that the Big Twenty-five would welcome some restraint on their competitive scramble so that they can settle down to the more serious exigencies of academic life than the hunt for celebrities. They should be able to build up, with competent if not famous staff, those areas sometimes overlooked in the race for fame. The pressures of high school graduates seeking admission to their golden portals might relax somewhat as the students apply to other schools which have achieved a minimum dignity. For the country at large, an intelligent redistribution of our academic resources would mean that more and more regions would have at least a generally good university, with all that this means in developing local physical, industrial, human, and cultural resources.

GRADUATE
SCHOOL:
THE TAIL
THAT WAGS
THE DOG?

WHAT single enterprise of a university is most likely to bring it fame and fortune today? Not its football team or its distinguished and wealthy alumni—although these, no doubt, continue to contribute their fair share. The graduate school does. The undergraduate colleges at Berkeley, Stanford, Harvard, or Columbia do not maintain the fabulous eminence of those institutions; their graduate schools do. This is true, in different ways and in varying degree, throughout the country.

No football victory can do as much for a university as a Nobel Prize bestowed on one of its professors, who is almost always on the graduate faculty; few private bequests can equal the largesse of the government or of a foundation which bestows a multimillion dollar grant, or of a corporation that awards a huge contract, on the basis of a university's academic prominence, a prominence inevitably measured by the achievements of the graduate school.

The graduate school has attained its dominating place in American higher education in spite of its relatively recent founding (in 1876, at Johns Hopkins), in spite of its having fewer students and faculty than undergraduate school, and in spite of widespread and sometimes nearly total disagreement, among faculty, students, and administrators, about its functions and operations. Jacques Barzun, when he was dean of the Graduate Faculties at Columbia, examined wisely and incisively many of the anomalies of American graduate education. His report, "Graduate Study at Columbia," together with Bernard Berelson's recent book *Graduate Education in the United States,* offer overwhelming testimony on the confusions, contradictions, and uncertainties under which graduate schools operate. The intentions of graduate school are often muddled; they are generally incompatible or irreconcilable with those of undergraduate colleges; sometimes they even cancel themselves out within the graduate school itself. Graduate school, as Dr. Barzun put it, is an amiable anarchy.

Yet its activities—the preparation of students for master's and doctor's degrees; the production of learned books and articles and scientific papers: that is, research and scholarship; the gathering of rare books and documents for the library; the bidding for money from government and foundation; the conducting of studies for industry—determine the values and character of undergraduate work, which still remains the main *raison d'être* of American universities. Even those colleges that offer no degrees beyond the bachelor's cannot escape the influence of the American graduate school. It may be no exaggeration to say that our graduate schools, at least indirectly, determine the whole character of American higher education today (and, by a filtering-down process, that of the high schools and elementary schools).

This is hardly a healthy situation, if only because it is so little recognized. It has developed so naturally that we are scarcely aware of it. We can readily see how graduate schools had to increase in size, scope, and number to meet the needs of the contemporary revolutions in science and technology. Undergraduate colleges, whose function still remains to a large extent the preparation of broadly educated persons, could not and still cannot meet the demands for highly trained specialists in physics, engineering, mathematics, or chemistry. Nor could the undergraduate colleges adequately satisfy all of the demands generated by the social revolution, among them providing the professors to meet the wish of more and more high school graduates for a college education. One of the earliest objectives of graduate schools was the preparation of college teachers in every discipline, and it remains a principal objective today.

No corner of American life is untouched by the graduate school. Without the graduate school, we would not have the chemists who made possible color film; the physicists and engineers who developed television; the engineers and designers who gave us jet planes; the biologists who developed antibiotics; the social workers and psychologists studying juvenile delinquency; the economists who suggest large and small ways for government, industry, and individuals to survive financially in the modern world; the literary critics who help us understand our literary culture; the unclassified thinkers who consider the effects of total war; the nuclear physicists who provide hints about the structure of matter; the anthropologists and sociologists who make us aware of our social existence; the theologians and philosophers who keep trying to find value and meaning in life; the historians and political scientists who put current events in a perspective of idea and facts; the accountants and merchandising specialists who run giant corporations. From our most practical and most public affairs to the most private and most abstract, the masters and doctors who have been to graduate school affect our lives.

This is not laboring the obvious even though everyone knows that educated men run our most important establishments today. But we forget or do not know that these men are not simply college graduates with baccalaureate degrees; they are experts who have developed their knowledge and talents in graduate school. (Those few who haven't actually been to graduate school have gone through a similar process of preparation.)

The mystery of how the graduate school has worked its wonders deepens when we look closely at the structure of graduate school, for we find almost at once that graduate school does not really exist. (I speak only of graduate schools that are part of universities. A few are independent, like Claremont Graduate School or the Harvard Graduate School of Business.) Graduate deans, for example, often have no budget except to pay secretaries and assistants. They do not hire, fire, or promote faculty (although their recommendations are certainly heeded); in fact, most graduate deans have no faculty. Graduate schools draw their faculty from departments. These departments, in turn, are constituent parts of colleges, Arts and Sciences, Engineering, Business Administration, Fine Arts, each of which has its own dean. Normally, chairmen of departments and deans of colleges hire, fire, and promote faculty, determine curriculum, fix budget, and otherwise run academic affairs. Graduate schools exist almost literally at the pleasure of "lesser" divisions although their pleasure, obviously, has been to make graduate schools bigger and better, sometimes indeed at the expense of undergraduate needs.

As graduate dean Roy Nichols, of the University of Pennsylvania, put it, "It seems only too apparent that the graduate dean, in certain instances, can be described as little more than a registrar and student counselor. Yet he and his part-time associates are responsible for the highest quality of university instruction and for the carrying out of some of the most difficult objectives of higher education."

Everything about graduate school—its curriculum, the training and interests of the faculty, its whole emphasis—

militates against its having harmonious relations with undergraduate work. Either it changes undergraduate work or is changed by it. Because of the present prestige of the graduate school, it almost always changes the undergraduate school.

Graduate schools must, first of all, depend on specialization. As one administrator put it, they concentrate on subject matter rather than on students. Undergraduate colleges, on the other hand, even education colleges and engineering schools, are dedicated to giving their students some kind of broad general education. The hope is to have the students learn something about a great many things, from painting to physics, as well as a good deal about one thing, the undergraduate "major." But the departmental arrangement of faculties, an arrangement dictated by the needs of the graduate school, makes it difficult to provide any integrating, broad knowledge except piecemeal. Departments guard the borders of their provinces jealously and zealously. A student of the 17th century in England, to get a full perspective of that time, would have to take courses in the departments of History, Art History, Music History, English, Philosophy, and perhaps Political Science, and even then the picture he gets would be a mosaic with thick lines.

The professor who ranges outside his area, who has "broad" interests, is likely to find no time or energy to be "deep," to explore his own area with the thoroughness expected of graduate professors. He is likely to be guilty of the academic heresy known as "dilettantism." A physics professor I know, profoundly interested in the history of science and the relation of science to art, literature, and music, was slightingly described to me by another physics professor as "an esthete." I heard a social science professor once wonder why an English teacher should be using Machiavelli's *The Prince* in a literature course. A specialist I know in contemporary American history has not read contemporary American writers: literature is "outside" his field.

These are perhaps extreme instances, but they are symptomatic. Also symptomatic are the difficulties undergraduate colleges encounter in setting up or administering interdisciplinary courses or curricula. When a new specialty does establish itself on the graduate or undergraduate level, like American Studies, many professors, with the best and most earnest will, often do not get the point. I attended the oral examination of an American Studies doctoral candidate, at which the sociologist asked about sociology, the political scientist about political science, the historian about history. Only two of the seven professors present asked questions that cut across departmental lines.

To study the interrelatedness of all human knowledge, the undergraduate college must consciously and forcefully introduce "general" programs. Many schools often do this, of course, and with such vigor and wisdom that their programs achieve considerable acclaim. Columbia College's undergraduate curriculum in Western Civilization, the interdepartmental honors programs now flourishing on many campuses, are among the more noteworthy attempts to bring breadth back into undergraduate study. But this is exactly the point: as graduate colleges build up their specializing role more and more, the undergraduate colleges must more and more deliberately assert their generalizing role. Most undergraduate colleges simply fall into the far easier pattern of paralleling the departmental isolationism of graduate school.

The graduate schools do not make conscious or explicit their control of undergraduate education; they cannot if only because they are subordinate. Occasionally, to be sure, demands are made in certain disciplines that students with baccalaureate degrees come completely prepared for highly advanced graduate work; this effectively prevents the students from doing more than the barest minimum of study outside the discipline. The demands of graduate schools simply pervade the atmosphere.

Graduate schools by their nature insist on "productive" work, not teaching alone or the turning out of scholars and scientists or other teachers, but the seeking after new knowledge and the offering to the world of the findings. Few undergraduate colleges can afford to ignore these standards of graduate school. One commonly applied measure in evaluating a college is the number of Ph.D.'s on its faculty; another is the number of publications the faculty can claim; a third is the number of volumes in the library. These measures are more relevant, obviously, to a graduate school than to an undergraduate one, but they are applied nevertheless to both. One consequence is that undergraduate departments are likely to arrange syllabi to suit graduate school needs. Many undergraduate catalogs are imitations of graduate school offerings. Professors look on introductory or interdepartmental courses as burdens draining their capacity for the searching and pioneering characteristic of graduate work.

If senior faculty in undergraduate colleges must live their professional lives under the scrutiny of the graduate school, their junior colleagues will actually be living in graduate school itself. Beginning instructors are almost always candidates for master's or doctor's degrees in a graduate school. They often cannot separate the demands made upon them to be specialists from those they make upon their own undergraduate students. Training of freshmen in footnote citation becomes a substitute for teaching the essence and substance of a subject. High school teachers of English drill their students in the niceties of reference, not simply perhaps because this is easier than emphasizing literacy, but

31

because manipulating scholarly apparatus has come to seem the first task of the student of English. Too often new and highly sophisticated approaches developed in graduate school plummet down even into elementary school, as when new mathematical, grammatical, or physical concepts are offered to children who may not be able to multiply numbers or to read.

The tensions that mark the graduate school's relation to undergraduate work are as nothing compared to the tensions within graduate school itself.

Much work in graduate school often has no relation at all either to teaching or to the pursuit of pure knowledge, enterprises normally associated with universities. To build up their financial and physical resources, many schools establish independent research units that conduct individual studies for government or industry. No attempt is made to mask the practical, profit-making aspect of these units. We often find the word "applied" modifying the "research." Some staff members do not teach or supervise graduate students; they are concerned exclusively with conducting research projects with very specific ends. And many universities encourage graduate staff to sign individual contracts to do such research; the "overhead" charges enrich the university's coffers.

Practically oriented research, whether carried on by individuals or by whole staffs, is likely to cast a depressing cloud of querulousness over the more usual work of a university, dedicated as it must be to the disinterested uncovering and dissemination of knowledge in every field. How must the study of Shakespeare and of Milton, of Latin and of Greek, of archeology and of paleontology, of any subject which will never elicit from corporation or government office a contract to come up with conclusions, seem to students and faculty engaged in it? The university has always had to resist the blandishments of the practical world of business and affairs, of course, and it has developed its defenses as necessary. But here we find it welcoming that world, making it at home on its own campus, a guest whose very presence challenges the values and activities and dedication of the host.

Berelson's book is a sober, thoroughly documented, exhaustive study of the internal stresses and strains of graduate school. Even someone who has a notion of the anarchy that prevails is appalled by the utter chaos recorded by Berelson. Time spent on doctoral degrees in the same subjects at different institutions may vary from four to eleven years; some candidates have spent nineteen years. The number of persons who have completed all but their dissertations is enormous. There is no substantial agreement anywhere about what the doctoral dissertation should be, whether it should be an exercise in scholarship or a genuine and substantial "contribution to learning." Some schools consider the doctorate a "research" degree; some as the "union card" for a professorial career. (Woodbridge, as quoted by Berelson: "Since the degree is conferred in Sanskrit and in animal husbandry, in philosophy and highway engineering, for what does it essentially stand?") Few administrators or students seem to know what the master's degree means anymore. Degrees in different subjects clearly require varying competence and preparation. In most institutions, the final oral examination for the doctor's degree is a mere formality, with no one failing. (Barzun: "Too often the scholarly degree is really a reward for the moral virtues of persistence and good will.") Many graduate students cannot write on a minimal level of decency. Most graduate students receive no sort of preparation for their first teaching jobs, being thrown into the classroom cold; most of them may not even know the material they are

33

supposed to teach, having taken only advanced courses in the subject. The instances of inconsistency, confusion, injustice, senselessness, disorder, waste, inefficiency, heartlessness, inconsiderateness, foolishness that mark graduate education in the United States may be multiplied endlessly, for new ones arise daily.

But having said all this, I must say that the fact is, simply, that the American graduate school does work, and remarkably well, although, obviously, it might be made to work better. The changes that seem to me to be needed are minimal. The American graduate school, which has no full parallel anywhere in the world, which has borrowed and improvised so freely without plan and often without apparent reason, which grew sporadically and spontaneously and continues to grow in the same way, reflects and meets peculiarly American needs. As Berelson puts it, "By and large, the graduate school is doing a reasonably good job or better, as judged by both the students and the employers." Most careful observers are agreed that the American graduate school is superior to the European, which, among other things, has fewer students, concentrates more on lectures and examinations, and is more concerned with turning out pure research specialists than teachers.

Some of the problems generated by the emergence of the graduate school in the United States can scarcely be blamed exclusively on it. They are the result of the whole structure of American education. If our high schools provided an appropriate broad education, as many do in Europe, then the undergraduate colleges could properly require a greater specialization, and the graduate schools could go about their even more highly intensified specialization with a clearer conscience. As it is, graduate schools worry no less intensely than the lower levels about how broad or how narrow graduate work should be. Many schools require their master's and doctor's candidates to offer minor as well as major fields. Only the post-doctoral student can today in most universities pursue a small subject with the thoroughness indispensable to becoming an expert in it and, hopefully, a discoverer or innovator.

Perhaps graduate school should be encouraged to become an even larger tail than it is so that it might wag the dog more effectively. What would seem to be needed is both a greater separation between graduate and undergraduate schools as well as a simultaneously greater integration. No paradox is involved, and some institutions have indeed worked out partial solutions along such lines. We still think of the graduate school as an appendage of the undergraduate college, and surely it is time to consider it a body in its own right, and one not less important. Dr. Barzun put it well when he called the graduate school "necessarily and properly the most expensive division of any university."

If graduate school did achieve a greater measure of independent status, some of the defects flowing from its present dependency might be minimized. We might recognize at once that some faculty members simply should not be expected to straddle undergraduate and graduate work. The duties, the dynamics, the talents, the energies are different in both areas although many of these obviously overlap. Not many professors are happy facing both freshman classes and doctoral seminars. To quote Barzun again: "One cannot convey to two hundred people in a room what one conveys to twenty."

Some of the colleges without graduate schools looming over them on their campuses have recognized that the efficacy of undergraduate teaching must be measured in other terms than "productivity"; they have tried to include criteria in evaluating staff that may be added to, or substituted for, research or scholarship, neither of which, of course, is unrelated to effective teaching. Many graduate professors work best with students in face-to-face or side-by-side situations; some are dismally disorganized lecturers or classroom teachers, and it is occasionally a cruelty to subject them to the conventional demands of undergraduate teaching.

A stronger graduate school could insist that its students not consider the work for a master's or doctor's degree as part-time, something to be pursued evenings only over long periods. Undergraduate schools offer scholarships more and more liberally; so might stronger graduate schools. If undergraduate colleges should pay students to get their degrees, as Margaret Mead has suggested, how much more urgent should it be for graduate schools to do the same. It should not be necessary for graduate students to teach in undergraduate college merely to subsidize themselves; they do not do much good for themselves with such work, and they are likely not to do freshmen much good either. High schools today would not think of hiring undergraduate college students to teach (except in extraordinary circumstances and under tight supervision); undergraduate colleges should develop a similar reticence (except for apprenticeship programs).

Graduate schools should choose their students with at least the same care as the quality undergraduate colleges do; they should not accept applicants with the barest qualifications. Many large graduate schools apparently cannot resist the financial benefits of admitting hordes for the master's degree. These students, even when they stay for only a year and do not complete their work, help subsidize the more serious work of graduate schools. But they also serve to adulterate the seriousness of that work. No professor should ever be made to feel that in return for being able to conduct a seminar for a handful of competent doctoral candidates, or to work alone in library or laboratory, he must perform before an audience of scores or hundreds of ill-prepared master's candidates.

A stronger, more independent, financially more secure graduate school (perhaps with its own endowment like an undergraduate college) would be able to accept or reject research contracts more independently, without having to consider irrelevant factors like "overhead" paid to the university which can be used to buy rare books in all fields or raise salaries of professors not so placed as to get lucrative contracts. Independent contract research is not out of place on a campus, and it is better in most cases for industry or government to come to the professor than for the professor to leave the campus and go to them. A university can use all findings, all knowledge, however practical or narrow; it knows what context in which to put discovery. If the graduate school can manage to achieve some substantial degree of separation from the undergraduate college, it can more readily allow itself to establish bureaus, institutes, centers to carry on directed research. It can improvise freely, even departing from the standard organization of universities when a project calls for a revolutionary originality. But only if it is strong and independent will it be able to balance and integrate its various activities with a sure sense that it is doing justice both to the university and the community. Only a strong school—and a secure professor—can be counted on to resist the pressures to come up with certain hoped for results.

Other benefits that would flow from a more independent, more important status for the graduate school suggest themselves readily enough. Graduate libraries could build the special collections needed for graduate work; graduate departments might be made more or less independent of undergraduate ones. With graduate schools relying so heavily

37

on undergraduate departments for their students and for their budgets, it is natural for the undergraduate chairman or dean to determine the level and character of the teaching the graduate student does in undergraduate classes. An independent graduate school, like a medical school, could more properly control the assignment of its students to periods of "clinical" or internship work, withholding them from departments where they are required to perform menial or irrelevant tasks. In general, it could more rigorously determine how to improve the preparation of graduate students for college teaching. In all matters, stronger graduate schools should be able to deal on a basis of equality with other units of a university.

An association of academically and financially strong graduate schools could more readily set their house in order, regularizing differences in standards and periods of study between disciplines and between schools. The difference between a B.A. from a good Mid-western college and one from a good Pacific or Atlantic Coast school is not very great, if it is discernible at all; that between M.A.'s or Ph.D.'s from two such institutions can be enormous. Undergraduate schools have long been systematically and rigorously organized into accrediting organizations; graduate schools still improvise temporary solutions to and meditate on the problems in their organizations, although the first steps toward systematic organization have been taken.

An independent graduate school could more hospitably welcome post-doctoral students to its facilities. Berelson lists a number of large institutions that are tacking onto their graduate schools centers for advanced study: MIT, Cal Tech, Illinois, Michigan, Chicago. Other schools are planning similar enterprises. All so far are in the sciences and social sciences. But these provisions often have to be makeshift since they must be subordinated to an already subordinated division. This is clearly a loss, for much important study can only be done on this highly advanced level.

Surely there can be nothing unfair or unbalanced in recognizing the central and predominant role graduate school now plays in American intellectual life. The graduate school has some while ago replaced the undergraduate college in this respect, yet the undergraduate college continues to expect the high schools to prepare students to meet its needs and expects the graduate schools to accept whatever it may offer them in the way of students and opportunities for research and teaching. It seems time for the graduate school to begin more vigorously, more consciously, more clearly determining the character of secondary and college education while at the same time it pursues its task of self-definition more boldly.

Learning and discovery, creation and invention, uncovering and ordering, analyzing and guiding, appreciation and evaluation, these have become the central concerns of American education. These are all the primary functions of graduate school. These supplement and build on the essential disseminating functions of the undergraduate colleges. The undergraduate colleges prepare students for life in general, not for specific jobs; when they pretend to make them professionals, they often prepare them for subordinate roles and set limits to their careers. Engineers, for example, without a liberal education and without graduate specialization, frequently cannot expect to rise above the level of engineering aides. This limitation is clearly seen in physics or mathematics, where no one expects the baccalaureate degree alone to prepare one for a career of genuinely significant study.

It seems to me right for graduate school to have taken on its varied tasks in American higher education. For if it had not done so, then undergraduate education would necessarily have had to become adulterated and fragmented as it tried to be both generalist and specialist. Undergraduate schools have enough to do to turn out properly schooled bachelors; this is an enormously important task in itself; they should not be expected also to assume the unique tasks involved in training masters and doctors and in advancing all fronts of knowledge. Undergraduate colleges spread knowledge; graduate schools do this too, of course, but always on the frontier, always in terms of enlarging knowledge while spreading it.

It's difficult to imagine the edifice of American education without the graduate school at the top. Nothing taught in elementary or high school or in college can come from elsewhere but the graduate school, in content, organization, or presentation. It is equally difficult to imagine American cultural and non-academic intellectual life without the American graduate school. Of course, a good deal of creative work and much work in the physical and social sciences are pursued federally and privately. But even in these areas, graduate school determines the character of the work and its presentation. Some such institutions without students simply model themselves in spirit and form on graduate schools, the Rockefeller Foundation, the Institute for Advanced Study, at Princeton, for example. When Saarinen designed the Bell Telephone Laboratories, he did so with the idea of a college campus in mind, and the pace and rhythm of the research pursued within the walls resemble most nearly those of a graduate school. Museums and private libraries (Folger, Huntington, Newberry) are often miniature graduate schools, in orientation and personnel. The findings of government and privately employed scientists, social scientists, and literary scholars are published alongside those of graduate school professors. Graduate school enclaves, in short, may be found in private industry, in Washington, D.C., at the headquarters of foundation enterprises, everywhere.

Perhaps it is time, then, to consider graduate school a whole dog in its own right and not just a tail to anything.

BRIDGING
THE TWO
CULTURES

JUST WHAT is a college education for today? The question is not new, nor has it gone begging for answers. But every so often it seems essential to answer it again in some detail, for it is at the heart of many more specific questions that keep coming up. We seem for some time now, in the middle of the 20th century, to have neglected giving a full answer to the question, unless we have indeed been giving it in hidden terms, in the arrangements we make on campuses, in the way we spend our money and distribute our honors. We seem to have been thinking of the answer in one way while acting it out in quite another.

American education has long ago accepted, both in word and deed, the primacy of a liberal undergraduate education. We widely agree that the bachelor's degree is not really intended to prepare one for a profession. Even when the degree is awarded in accountancy or in engineering or in elementary education, fields in which it is possible to step into a job immediately after commencement, the curriculum clearly calls, almost universally, for some two years of courses in the "humanities," however these may be defined. We accept that a college degree without some content in literature, philosophy, the arts, history, as well as in science and in social science, is not likely to indicate that the holder of it is "educated," that is, that he has developed a sense of the range and depth and complexity of human experience, knowledge, and wisdom.

Yet, in spite of this generous gesture toward liberal education, we find that in practice the tendency is to neglect the humanities and allied fields, to push for a narrowing rather than a broadening of undergraduate education, to drop "useless" courses and to add "useful" ones. No more dramatic instance of this neglect can be offered than the distribution of federal funds to higher education. In 1961, the government appropriated some $563 million for colleges and universities. Of the total, 99 per cent went to the natural and physical sciences, including agriculture, and the remaining 1 per cent to the social sciences. Not a penny went to the humanities. During the same period much was heard from Washington about the importance of our national culture. Millions of words for theater, poetry, and music, but not a cent to encourage or support them. We continue saying one thing, we do another.

Gordon N. Ray, Secretary General of the Guggenheim Foundation, summed up the situation in a recent speech, "Is Liberal Education Still Needed?": "The non-liberal aspects of the academic program have come to be the principal reasons for the university's prestige both with its students and with the outside world."

It is perhaps no wonder that the 19th century debate between scientist and humanist, between Huxley and Arnold, should have broken out anew today, between Sir Charles Snow and Dr. F. R. Leavis, with all the rancor and confusion of an altogether new argument. It's as though we had not ever brooded over the question of what a college education is for, as though the answer had not already long ago been worked out to emphasize humanism, liberalism, broad rather than narrow scientific or technological professionalism. It

43

may well be that we ought to look hard at our traditional answer in behalf of humanism, for while we may not want to abandon its surface formulation, we seem to be wearing away at its foundation. If we do not want to plunge into the gulf between the two cultures of science and humanism, we should try to bridge them.

It is not an extreme statement of the case to say that the emphasis in higher education today is on practically oriented work. The research that may be applied to immediately recognizable ends is supported. Theoretical physics and mathematics are encouraged because they are related to atomic physics or missile study, not because they are related, as they were once seen to be, to Sanskrit or Egyptology. Those fields of sociology, economics, psychology, anthropology are booming which can be adapted to "practical" ends in our society. In English, technical writing is a growing field.

We have been moving steadily toward the practical. More and more the issue is put bluntly: college is not supposed to educate one; it is supposed to prepare one for a job. I have attended faculty meetings at which physical scientists and engineers have fought vigorously to keep their students from taking other than "practical" courses. The objection was that forcing students to follow the usual sequence of liberal arts courses would increase the time necessary to complete the professional training requisite for a job. On many campuses, whenever a conflict develops between having students enroll in required liberal or required professional courses, the decision is almost always in favor of the professional. The rationale, sometimes stated, generally understood, is that the latter will help the student get a job.

Even when arguments are made in favor of liberal education, they are made in terms of the practical, of the benefits of a liberal education in a job. The Fund for Adult Education collected in a booklet statements by business leaders and others urging the value of a liberal education, *Toward the Liberally Educated Executive.* The dominant theme is that liberal education has "job" value: "The qualifications needed for leadership in industry are developed largely through a liberal arts education. . . . In more and more companies, the decisive factor is going to be the breadth and depth of executive judgment. . . . On one point all authorities have agreed. Narrow specialization is not enough; this is already responsible for most of the inability of middle management executives to be considered for promotion. . . . The study of the *humanities*—of literature, art, and philosophy, and of the critical terms that these disciplines use to assess the world—is startlingly more pertinent and practical than the 'practical' vocational preparation. . . . It can be said with little exaggeration that of the common college courses being taught today the ones most nearly 'vocational' as preparation for management are the writing of poetry and of short stories."

In short, liberal education is good business. It shows a profit. It helps you get ahead. At the moment, American industry and business, and perhaps even American public and intellectual life, seem to be in need of at least some liberally educated men in addition to the technicians. As the colleges and universities have met the need in the past for a supply of specialists, so they may now be expected to meet the need for generalists. (The need for liberally educated men is not nearly so great as that for physicists and engineers, for we are seeing very little pouring into the universities of funds to support teaching and research in the classical languages or in literature or in the arts.)

The arguments made out for a liberal education by our business leaders emphasize how thoroughly we have changed our answer to the question of what a college education is for. At one time, as we know from reading the texts of the artists and philosophers of Western civilization, education had to do with living in the fullest sense. We could comfortably grant that beauty was its own end, art its own justification, knowledge its own pleasure. Now we argue that education has to do with profits. The answer to La Place's question about *Phèdre*, "What does it prove?" as Gordon Ray reminds us, was once, "It proves nothing but itself." Now the answer is, "It may help you become vice-president of your company."

A. E. Housman crystalized the issue eloquently. "Knowledge resembles virtue," he said, "in this, and differs in this from other possessions, that it is not merely a means of procuring good, but is good in itself simply: it is not a coin which we pay down to purchase happiness, but has happiness indissolubly bound up with it." Further, Housman argued, "once we have recognized that knowledge in itself is good for man, we shall need to invent no pretext for studying this subject or that. . . . Other desires perish in their gratification, but the desire of knowledge never: the eye is not satisfied with seeing nor the ear filled with hearing."

I do not ask at all that we return to some golden age of the past, for I do not believe there ever was such an age. When students did pursue learning according to the ideal of Housman, there were fewer students, the world was simpler, our horizons smaller. It happens that I was able myself, briefly, to live by Housman's noble ideal. It was during the Great Depression of the 'thirties, when no school work had any practical end, and it never occurred to most of us to stop to justify in terms of usefulness our study of Latin or Greek or calculus. (So unrealistic was that world that I was advised by a faculty counselor at least to keep in mind the possibility of a career and not to major in mathematics, which he thought would never offer as many opportunities for a livelihood as English.) But a depression is hardly a golden age.

46

I ask, rather, that we consider Housman's answer to the question *as well as* the answer given by the business leaders. Both answers are essential in the modern world. If we live only by the practical answer, we can get into trouble quickly. Today, for example, students are encouraged to study Latin because it is supposed to help one with English vocabulary and grammar, with foreign languages, with scientific and pharmaceutical terms. (Such reasoning makes me squirm, for I am one of those persons who find it easier to remember, say, telephone numbers by the score rather than gimmicky little jingles which are supposed to help one remember telephone numbers.) One can far more readily learn scientific vocabulary, the rules of English grammar, and foreign languages directly rather than through the medium of Latin, although, of course, Latin may be helpful. Students quickly realize this and if they have been conned into studying Latin because of its supposed fringe benefits, they abandon their efforts. The same is true, I venture, of potential business executives. If the end of liberal education is merely to help one get ahead on the job, there are more direct and more efficient ways of accomplishing this end. Short-term, capsule courses in "The Great Works of Western Man," Dale Carnegie-like instruction, even do-it-yourself cultural enterprises (like paintings, symphonies, or books-of-the-month clubs), may serve as effectively as a full four-year undergraduate curriculum culminating with a baccalaureate in Latin or French. Some companies do actually establish dehydrated, "blitz" programs in the humanities in the hope of civilizing their executives fast.

No, the object of liberal education must continue in substantial measure to remain itself. It is its own good, its own end, its own justification. At least one contributor to the symposium on liberally educated executives suggested this. "A man is free, or he enjoys liberty," Ralph Barton Perry wrote, "in the proportion to which his life is governed by his own *choice*. And choice itself is a matter of degree; for it may be wide or narrow, deep or shallow. Choice is narrowed by ignorance, habit, or obsession; it is broadened by knowledge, spontaneity and reflection. . . . Education is liberal in so far as it invites and qualifies men to choose deeply and fundamentally, to choose ends as well as means, to choose remote as well as immediate ends, to choose from many rather than from few possibilities." As Ray said: "Specialized training deals with what is 'right,' liberal education with what is 'true.' "

Because of the widening gulf in our time between the two cultures of humanism and science, we tend to forget that liberal education includes the best of both cultures. Liberal education embraces not only the humanities; it embraces the sciences and social sciences. The defining quality of liberal education is that it can have no limits of any sort. It even includes purely practical work (although we sometimes justify our practical pursuits in terms of "hobbies"—photography, woodworking, automobile repair). Its end is to stimulate and satisfy all curiosity.

Ray quotes Thomas Huxley on this issue: "It would be as great a scandal that any person possessing a University degree in Arts should be ignorant of the law of gravitation, or of the chemical fact that air is not an element . . . or of the circulation of blood in his own body . . . as that a B.Sc. should be ignorant of Cromwell's existence." Or, to put it another way, liberal education is a balanced education.

Professionalists simply do not understand this point. To them advocates of liberal education are dilettantes. This is as true of as many professors in the humanities as in the pure and applied sciences. The professionalists fight against teaching "service" courses, that is, courses taken by students not majoring in the subject. They do not want to integrate knowledge; they want to compartmentalize it. They see only the difficulties of synthesis, none of the possibilities. Their vision is narrowed by blinders; they are like members of medieval guilds in their exclusiveness.

The debate between Snow and Leavis resolves itself, in at least one dimension, to that between liberal and professional education. Are colleges and universities in the West to turn out engineers and scientists to guide our civilization, or philosophers and humanists? Snow's answer, in part, is simply that liberal education has lost for itself the right to speak for our total culture. "What he seems to require for scientists," as Lionel Trilling put it, commenting on the Leavis-Snow controversy, "is the right to go their own way *with no questions asked*. The culture of literature, having done its worst, must now be supplanted and is not ever to play the part of a loyal opposition."

Snow's argument against the culture of literature (to simplify it grossly), which is to say, I think, against the culture characterized by liberal education, is based, peculiarly, on the same premise as the argument directed against science and technology. He intimates that liberal education with its disregard for the practical, for the very real daily needs of mankind, is in essence callous, is indifferent to man. He intimates, for example, that liberal education led to Auschwitz. The scientific, technological, practical culture of the Western world, on the other hand, has been concerned with specific improvements in man's daily world. It has produced antibiotics, raised standards of living, reduced pain, increased longevity, opened new possibilities for happiness for multitudes.

The argument between Snow and Leavis, of course, concerns itself with larger issues than just these, but in one way or another, as much in its implications as in its actual points of issue, it resolves itself into a controversy between hu-

49

manist and scientist. The issue between Snow and Leavis, however, should come down not to which culture should be dominant in our civilization today but rather to the one of how best to integrate the two cultures. Surely the excesses of misunderstanding committed by both Snow and Leavis in their public discussion are evidence enough of the gulf between professional scientist and professional humanist. But this gulf is only of recent development. Lionel Trilling points this out. "Sir Charles mentions Faraday among those scientists who overrode the limitations of social class to form the 'scientific culture' of England," he writes. "This is true only so far as it can be made consonant with the fact that Faraday could not have imagined the idea of a 'scientific culture' and would have been wholly repelled by it. It is told of Faraday that he refused to be called a *physicist;* he very much disliked the new name as being too special and particular and insisted on the old one, *philosopher,* in all its spacious generality: we may suppose that this was his way of saying that he had not overridden the limiting conditions of class only to submit to the limitations of profession.... From his belief in Mind, he derived the certitude that he had his true being not as a member of this or that profession or class, but as—in the words of a poet of his time—'a man speaking to men.' "

The trouble in the modern world, of course, is that we can no longer readily afford the luxury of educating philosophers who choose to practice physics. The science of physics requires so much preparation, in mathematics principally but also in chemistry, and has grown so enormously, that a student must spend very nearly all of his time, as an undergraduate and graduate, taking only courses in his field. This is true, of course, of other areas, in science, in medicine, in technology.

I think it futile to resist this reality. Our time does need specialists in areas which demand dedication over long periods. We might ease the total situation somewhat by requiring more work in the high schools in preparation for some contemporary careers; certainly the teaching of higher levels of mathematics has been taken on by the high schools over the last century. We might content ourselves with turning out less than the well-grounded physicist or engineer in four years of college, expecting that graduate school will finish the work. But these are makeshift responses and they do not, I think, quite acknowledge the proper importance of both professional and liberal education.

We must first concede that American higher education today does have a practical intention. We are no longer simply teaching the sons of gentlemen to enter the society of their upper-class families. Higher education, in England as well as in the United States, has long ago spread out from Gothic, ivy campuses to modern, red-brick ones. The students have to consider making a living; the country, for all of the money it invests in higher education, must expect that national needs be met.

We have acknowledged this twofold character of American higher education in various ways. The first two years of college have traditionally been devoted to a broad spectrum of courses, where students find their strengths and weaknesses and where they presumably determine their fields of specialization, which they enter in the last two years. The first two years offer the basic liberal education. Professional courses are now sometimes begun by students in their third or fourth undergraduate years. These substitute for the major, enabling the student to get his undergraduate degree after the usual fourth year of study, and his professional degree after another two or three years instead of, say, after a full four years. Some dentistry schools are doing this although some urge their applicants to get a full undergraduate major in some field unrelated to dentistry. Some law schools will allow students to start their law work in the senior undergraduate year, the law courses counting toward the undergraduate major. Such arrangements are not altogether new; they used to characterize a good deal of professional training.

The history of professional education in America—the movement away from allowing physicians, dentists, and lawyers to concentrate on their professional training alone, to requiring them first to have a full four-year undergraduate course, back to a mixing of the two—emphasizes the American tendency to blend the "practical" with the "cultural."

But I question the efficacy of having the student move from one territory of study to another across a sharp dividing line. One day the student's education stops and his training begins. The law student closes his texts in history and philosophy and literature and begins poring over tomes in law; the medical student abandons the study of Man and begins the study of men, in the form first of cadavers. Yet the main characteristic of liberal education is that it never really stops. Might it not be much more meaningful for every student to continue his liberal education simultaneously with his professional one? The liberal courses would certainly enrich the professional ones: consider how related would be, say, the study of history or political philosophy to a law school course in contracts or legal procedure; or one in Shakespeare or in contemporary drama to a medical school course in psychiatry.

The point in any arrangement to combine liberal with professional education on a vertical, side-by-side basis is that the two cultures must be dynamically integrated. The missile scientist who is illiterate in the area of human art and speculation may be at some moment in history a greater danger to mankind than a poet ignorant of Newton, for the missile scientist will surely be more intimately involved in momentous decisions than the poet. But in the largest perspective, even if we leave out the men who count backwards from ten or who press buttons or who advise others on when to do these things, it seems to me a serious loss for residents in either culture to be ignorant of the character and values and language and some of the substance in the other. The student of literature who is also taking courses in physics (or in any science) will understand literature in a richer context than if he immersed himself exclusively in literature; scarcely a period of man's history fails to show an intimate enmeshing of science with art. Sir Charles feels that pioneering in science should be as proper a subject for dinner conversation among educated persons as recent literature or politics, and I agree with him. (My own experience, however, has been that most humanists are more likely to be able to talk about scientific matters than most scientists about literary ones.)

An interpenetration of liberal with professional education would not only keep alive and alert one's sense of their actively symbiotic relationship; it would make it impossible to lose one's sense of idiom, so to speak, in one or the other. The humanist or social scientist who last worked in physics or calculus as a sophomore is not likely to retain throughout his graduate career that sense of strategy, of dynamics, that characterizes those fields. The scientist who has last read poetry as a sophomore has difficulty once he enters upon his career understanding even the vocabulary of a new poet. (A physician I know once remarked to me with a baffled sadness that he thought he could understand poetry pretty well, but now that he has found time to read again, he wonders whether he ever did.) It is difficult to go

53

back and explore another culture happily and profitably once we have become aliens from it for a period.

More importantly, much more importantly, we live in an integrated world, where only extremists find that the gulf between scientist and humanist cannot be bridged. Perhaps the humanist is more likely to be at fault here, for the civilized scientist keeps acknowledging that he has humanity in mind all the time; hopefully, the last of our barbaric scientists vanished with the Nazis. The scientist must be humanist, or we shall have Huxley's *Brave New World,* Orwell's *1984.* The humanist must understand science, or he will continue to be frightened and outraged by the scientist. The bridge between the two cultures must allow passage both ways.

No doubt practical difficulties will present themselves in working out any such vertical integration as proposed, but some law and medical schools have already started exploring possibilities of this sort. Certainly the problem is eased on campuses where there is a sense of larger community among the liberal and professional departments.

College, of course, is finally only one small area for liberal education. Such education should ideally begin early, certainly not later than high school, and, if set into proper motion, it will continue late, throughout life. The momentum of a liberal education never runs down. College is simply a comfortable, hospitable shelter for examining with intensity some of the content and principles of the world's wisdom and creations. Liberal education is co-terminous with living itself.

WHY I DON'T
WEAR MY
PHI BETA KAPPA
KEY

MY ELECTION to Phi Beta Kappa was a great day for me. I was given a present of a watch chain (although I had no watch), I got a suit with a vest, and I lost little time displaying the key across my front. There wasn't much occasion to wear it, for not long after, I found myself in an army uniform, which comes without a vest of course. When I left the service and began looking for a job, I got another suit with a vest and again hung my key across it. I remained proud but self-conscious about wearing the key. Once, when a prospective employer remarked about it, I modestly waved it away. He stopped me. "No, no," he said, "I respect the key very much. You should wear it without apology. It means a great deal."

It did mean a great deal to me, in private even more than in public. I framed my certificate of membership. I subscribed to the Phi Beta Kappa society's publication, *The American Scholar*, the first periodical I had ever subscribed to, and I read it faithfully. Even so I had vague suspicions that the key did not fully represent everything I thought it did. I remember squirming, as though the joke were directed at me, when a fool appeared in a college skit wearing a gigantic replica of the key that went from his chin to his knees. If I had been less green, less self-satisfied, and perhaps more honest, I would have earlier formulated my doubts. As it was, I wore the key less and less, as the result of a normal forgetfulness and indifference, until, like other items of costume jewelry, it got lost and I stopped wearing it altogether. It's found now, and it's attached by a short leather strap to a pocket watch, but I wear it rarely, still largely out of indifference, I must say, but a little out of principle. For I have become somewhat ashamed of announcing that I am a member of the society.

When I first got the key, I was completing a liberal education. I had majored in English and taken Latin. My interests were catholic. I had considered majoring in mathematics or physics, and I was intensely aware of the issues in the social sciences. Most importantly, perhaps, I tried to be conscious of my study of literature in the larger contexts of art (the relation with painting, sculpture, architecture, music, cinema, drama) and of thought (the ties with history, anthropology, sociology, philosophy, psychology, and so on). The key was a sign to me not only that I had worked through a good introduction to liberal education, but that it was important to have done so.

While I did not respect immodesty or ostentation, I also felt that a discreet assertion of what was truly important was not wrong. Some of the professors who wore their keys were men I admired for their wisdom, their breadth, their air of civilization; they were unself-conscious about displaying the key. *The American Scholar* reflected a humane, serious yet balanced concern with important subjects; it was not apologetic about being intellectual, informed, sober, broad. In spite of my self-consciousness, I wore the key with pride. It has been the only such statement I have ever worn. And while I don't wear it now, I still think frivolous the conventional objection to any display of affiliation or belief; I have never despised, as my non-conformist friends have done, men with Masonic or Rotarian pins or tiny crucifixes or stars of David in their lapels. Some persons find it more necessary than others to define themselves for the outside world, and that's their business.

But I was uneasily aware that a few of my professors wore the key under false pretenses. They and a number of my new fraternity brothers seemed to make up the largest class of key wearers I knew then or know now. They did not think; they did not read; they did not discuss. There was no evidence that they were in any way aware of the life of the mind. At the time, I supposed that winning the key marked the height of their intellectual careers, as Christian Darling's eighty-yard run in a practice football session in college marked the height of his athletic career, in Irwin Shaw's story, and that there was reason for their sad decline. They flashed the key because it was all that was left of their early career. I assumed that the key had once meant the same thing to them as it had to me.

When I entered the academic world and met other members of PBK, I realized that I had been too generous. It became clear that many of the most ostentatious key wearers never had understood what the key meant in the world at large. For them it meant that they had proved themselves in one spurt; they had performed one moderately spectacular feat. Admission into PBK was the end of a career instead of the beginning of one. Their arrogance was empty even of memory.

It is perhaps inevitable that such a type should develop. Election to PBK is almost entirely a matter of statistics. (Chapters eliminate beforehand students of clearly dubious character, like rapists and thieves.) If your grade average in your senior or junior year, or on graduation, is high enough, election is in most places automatic. This seems proper, for if the candidate has pursued a liberal undergraduate curriculum which has ranged widely, then his grades are likely to be as good an index as any of how much he has learned. Justice will more safely be served if the standard for election remains largely objective; the irrelevant considerations of heredity, family background, or belief that guide election to purely social fraternities cannot be used to blackball candidates for PBK. The obvious danger is that the student who is merely a grade hound will inevitably be elected to PBK, and this seems to be exactly what at least this most obvious class of PBK key wearers were.

There is something sad about this class. Whatever motives inspired these students to hunt greedily for grades in the first place, avoiding courses and teachers that would not all but guarantee them A's and B's, must also inspire them to wear the key after graduation. They still hunt for the A's and B's of the world. Their achievement is not a private matter, a source of private satisfaction or pleasure; it is the basis only for public display. They are so little sensitive to the effect of their bearing and appearance that they are oblivious to the contradiction between the key and their lives. They are oblivious to the shabby spectacle they present; Christian Darling as football hero manqué at least learned to doubt himself.

A second, smaller class of key wearers is made up of the smart alecks, those who wear the key but deride it. These are likely to be the same cynics who sneer at their diplomas, hanging them in their bathrooms; they brightly and cattily lampoon all values, all attainment, all serious work. They travel in packs, gaining strength from their own company, reinforcing their tiny superiorities. They are intelligent enough, no doubt, and even amusing, but they are finally no less sad than the smug and stupid key wearers, for they know better than to believe that election to PBK is an end in itself. They are clearly embarrassed by their brethren.

But they have no positive sense of their own of the meaning of the key; they apprehend dimly that it should mean more than it does, and so they wear it. In the company of their fellows, however, they must also reject it, for they sense that it also means less. They are both in and out.

The least objectionable type of PBK key exhibitor no doubt is the one who continues his life in the heart of the humane civilization symbolized by PBK but is totally unaware of anyone, both those out of his world altogether or in it uncertainly. Perhaps this type has more profound things to be concerned about than the sociology of PBK key wearers, and, if so, all honor to him. It is perhaps more likely that he is simply unaware of the landscape, indifferent, narrow; his life smells of the candle and of the library. His liberal education is bounded, walled in, by his professional interests; he is parochial; his peripheral world is blanked out.

I suppose one may find other types of key wearers. However, I am not interested in definitiveness here but in characterizing the main groups I have known in order to make a point about the PBK society as a whole. That is, simply, that the society does not really stand in the modern world for liberal humanism in the largest, hardest, deepest, most exciting sense; it stands for it in the narrowest, tightest, most sterile, most superficial, and dullest sense.

Now, obviously, this is a sweeping charge and there are so many PBK members we all know who violate this generalization that it would seem hardly supportable. Let me just say that if the majority of PBK members, who, I submit, do not wear their keys, many for reasons like mine, were to become active in the society, then surely it might revive its original concern with the full life of the mind and of the senses. As the society stands today, however, it has as its largest groups of active and publicly proclaimed members the three types I have described. No doubt these types will always continue to wear the key, and any other insignia they may earn, but it happens that today they are in accord with the spirit of the society as it expresses itself formally. They are a composite of contemporary Phi Beta Kappa man.

Meetings of PBK chapters, when they do not involve some ritual of self-congratulation, avoid significant issues. Speakers and their subjects are generally chosen by someone living in the musty, insulated, artificial, and pleasant enough world of Mr. Pickwick or Mrs. Grundy, not designed exactly to satisfy very deep needs of thought or feeling. When a chapter finds itself considering a living question, it will more often than not do so with a stunning naivete. I once watched in astonishment as a New York chapter allowed a clique to take over a meeting, at which the distinguished speaker was kept waiting, so that resolutions might interminably be passed supporting some momentary cause.

"PBK members mature too early," a colleague once remarked to me. "They take the values of undergraduate life as all important. When they go out into the world of genuine performance, of shifting standards, the world of infinite variety in its demands and rewards, they become lost. The world as a whole too often has different and more capacious requirements than those of the university. In the arts, the sciences, the social sciences, in the world or in the academy, how many of the brilliant men were PBK as undergraduates? A great many, no doubt, but not nearly all; not nearly the majority is my impression. Undergraduate PBK's sometimes simply exhaust their energies before graduation; some have never had the particular energies for distinction outside the classroom." Of course, the society recognizes the late starter and bestows honorary membership on persons who distinguish themselves after graduation. (Sometimes,

60

of course, the election is virtually automatic, as when faculty members reach a certain status.) But honorary members are often not active ones; they are not the ones who live within the society on a regular basis. Most regular members, when they bother to be active within the society at all, seem to require of it only that it not disturb them, that it not stimulate the glands or the brain, that it function as another weekly bridge or poker or sewing circle.

The truly civilized man must always work to remain what he is. He must keep up a receptive, alert, sweeping awareness of the world around him, and this awareness must be sensitive, uncommitted, flexible, unguided by mechanical expectations; it must not be screened by a barrier of taboos which limit apprehension. The best qualities of the American scholar of the 20th century are those which enable him to study all experience, all possibility, with freshness and seriousness in the setting of a fully informed sense of the past. He is free of the bindings of prejudice, of ignorance, of insensitivity, of shallowness of thought and feeling, of all of the inadequacies which limited the intellectual aristocrat of the past. The perspective of the modern American scholar remains large; he abandons none of the important values and he does not become obsessed by trivia; he does not vitiate his expansive, rich idealism with a defensive vindictiveness against irritating but petty realities. He is not stuffy, cranky, intolerant, uncharitable, ungenerous, supercilious; he is not absolute about the simpler certainties, those regarding details of bearing or of content. As we consider the figure of the Phi Beta Kappa man today, however, he seems to be in sum everything he should not be.

For example, in setting up the criteria for admitting new chapters, the national society has a good deal to say about an institution's athletic policy. I had always thought good and proper the principle of not allowing a chapter to be established on a campus which favors athletics to the actual detriment of liberal education. Measuring the quality of a college (by counting Ph.D.'s, books in the library, etc.) is a perfectly sensible thing to do. But PBK policy does not have so simple and positive an intention; it has set out, with a thin-lipped Puritanical emphasis on the negative, to refuse chapters to universities and colleges which do not exalt liberal arts *over* athletics. Its attitude toward athletics seems to me to crystalize its attitude toward the world at large.

The official policy of PBK was put not long ago baldly as follows: "If an institution awards to athletes scholarships and other financial assistance in larger sums, either in total or in individual grants, than to other undergraduates, it does not encourage scholars and scholarship with equitable generosity." Obviously this is true, but any number of state institutions, compelled by all sorts of circumstances quite beyond their control and having nothing to do with the internal character of the university, must support *both* athletics *and* scholarship. What PBK was saying is that no matter how generously a university supports learning and scholarship, even if this means as generously as Harvard itself, or even more generously, it will not get a chapter of PBK if it also supports athletics, or even one athlete, even more generously. One patently ridiculous consequence has been that small liberal arts colleges, many of them girls' schools, a number of them in the boondocks of the Bible Belt, with small athletic programs, or none at all, and with equally small programs of support to scholarship and learning, or no support at all, have been getting PBK chapters in recent years while larger, state supported institutions with larger athletic *and* larger scholarship programs, have been denied chapters.

Such a policy seems designed to cut off one's nose to spite

one's face; its end is the opposite of its intention. Which institutions, for example, have emphasized liberal learning and have more clearly recognized scholarly achievement, the universities of Michigan, Wisconsin, Oregon, Illinois, Iowa, Oklahoma, all with famous football teams, or such centers of learning and scholarship as Chatham College, Fordham University, Hollins College, Lake Forest College, Scripps College? The first group might well find itself without chapters of Phi Beta Kappa if current standards were applied; the second group is of institutions recently admitted to membership.

The evidence is certainly strong that an extravagant athletic policy can hurt learning and scholarship, but it is equally strong that an astute, sophisticated university administration can work out ways of balancing the demands of the outside world to have athletics with those of the inside to support learning and scholarship. Much of the money that goes for athletics in many states would never go to the university for purposes of education. The skilled administrator tries not so much to eliminate athletics as to improve learning and scholarship; the two need not be mutually exclusive. Surely the state universities of California, at Los Angeles and Berkeley, have demonstrated conclusively that strong football teams do not have to mean weak faculties or weak student bodies.

What Carthage was to Cato, athletics is to PBK. Whatever other force may threaten liberal education, athletics must be destroyed first. At the same time that the national society affirmed the statement of policy on athletics cited above, it rejected a resolution proposing that it deny charters to any public or private institution that excluded students from admission to it "on account of race." One need hardly remark that if athletic policy is harmful to learning and scholarship, surely an admission policy based on any sort of segregation is at least as harmful. For that matter, the question might also be appropriate of an institution's denominational commitment, which might conceivably bar or control learning and scholarship in certain areas.

I do not wish to argue with PBK on the merits of any of these particular issues. I am more concerned with the attitude of mind and spirit which PBK reveals with something like its athletic policy. As I read it, it reveals a humanism that has become sterile, that is unaware of the largest context of our society, that has become self-righteous and inflexible. It betrays a failure, I think, to understand even the original thrust of establishing PBK chapters, which was not simply to "reward" an institution or a student, but to bestow a sign upon students and institutions actively participating in the enterprises of liberal learning and scholarship. Generations of students who have in every way fulfilled the demands of a liberal education and have dedicated themselves to the way of life symbolized by Phi Beta Kappa are denied whatever honor there remains in election to the society. (I confess that I speak with a particular bitterness here, for I have seen brilliant students in the humanities, who were granted Woodrow Wilson Fellowships, and went on to earn their doctorates, denied PBK membership because of the caprice of the national society.)

An enlightened, living, truly liberal and humane philosophy could not settle so rigidly, with such stiff-backed arrogance, on any main or negative standard for exclusion. I am not suggesting that standards of excellence be abandoned or adulterated. But excellence is a many-faceted phenomenon today; the broader its base, the more meaningful it is. The study of Greek and Latin, still exalted by Phi Beta Kappa in its scholarship grants, was once at the center of liberal learning, for it included literature, philosophy, and even science. It is at least a little anachronistic to continue

64

exalting Greek and Latin for similar reasons today; their study, however noble and however much to be encouraged, is at best on the edge of things. To believe that they are central is simply to betray one's antiquarianism, to confess to a love of the past simply for the past, not for its values and glory. Humanistic study today by no means excludes classical study, but it does center on other areas, literature in the vernacular, for one, on philosophy in the modern world, on the nature and strategies of science, on sociology and anthropology, on history as it continues to surge vitally into the immediate present. And one need hardly say again that the civilized men of the ancient world believed in the whole man: a sound mind in a sound body.

A love of the past without a consciousness, an understanding, and a love of the present is not merely reactionary, it is likely to be mushy. It is decadent, self-indulgent, taking easy and automatic escape routes away from difficulties. It is soft and sentimental for all of its seeming toughness; it misunderstands the past, distorts the present. It sees all things as they are wished to be, not as they were or are. It does not want actually to keep what is best in the past and what is best in the present; it wants simply, like any reactionary political or social philosophy, to legislate or blackmail conformity with itself, twisting arms, force-feeding, doing anything short of applying the lash or the bastinado.

I exaggerate, of course. I speak of a tendency, an impulse, a tone, more than of a total actuality. Within Phi Beta Kappa itself are forces trying to make it come alive. No national meeting of the society passes without someone speaking up with some vigor about the athletic policy, which has even been called "hypocritical" out loud. The athletic policy cited above has been revised so as to give at least some consideration to the total stance of a university.

The American Scholar, considering its limitations of resources, does a remarkable job keeping on top of important, current issues. At best, it is as tough-minded, as lambent, as revelatory as any writing today. The spirit of free discussion does animate the society and its individual chapters, and one can still talk out on any subject—whether or not he has an interested audience. Perhaps one should not even charge the society with some fault of commission so much as one of omission. Those members who might agitate it into some meaningful activity are busy elsewhere, having given up working within the society, which occupies so remote a place from the center of the world's main and best activity. Obviously this is unfortunate, for the society is still perhaps the most proper forum for asserting the peculiar need for liberal education today; it remains the obvious parliament for bringing about more than a merely formal rapprochement between the two cultures of science and humanism.

The place of PBK in American life is a subject deserving of some passion, I think. The celebration of liberal study must continue to be a private affair; it must bestow its own pleasures and its own rewards, and these must be individually recognized, asserted, and supported. Liberal learning must never become frozen, dogmatic, moribund; it must remain alive. Otherwise love of it is a form of necrophilia. The national society and the individual chapters might do well to consider how to revitalize the cadaver.

"We are not a fraternity that lets people in," an ancient of PBK once snorted to me, "we keep them out." But PBK is not a campus social society maintaining exclusiveness by an invidious snobbery. It is not a society of genteel, tea-sipping Brahmins, meeting to gossip about their superiority to untouchables. Instead of seeking ways of excluding more and more students dedicated to liberal learning, PBK ought to be finding ways of identifying them anywhere and of including them. The process established by the national society to examine applying institutions for eligibility is so cumbersome and so costly that it serves effectively by itself to limit the number of new chapters. Seemingly qualified chapters are simply passed over each examining period without even being considered. Certainly it would not be amiss for the society to seek foundation aid to subsidize the process of selection if it is interested in vigorously supporting learning and scholarship everywhere (let alone in demonstrating a concern with elementary justice, one of the important humane virtues).

The issue may be summed up simply. The cause of PBK can best be served only by a broadly based and active membership, not by a narrow, quiescent one. Any student or scholar anywhere who properly belongs to the society but is not in it is another person lost to the cause. The privilege of wearing a Phi Beta Kappa key becomes no privilege at all if those entitled to wear it will not do so or cannot through no fault of their own. I myself shall never feel comfortable wearing the key until I know that all other persons entitled to wear it have been invited to do so.

Let the society indeed rise *per aspera ad astra,* in accordance with its motto, like the phoenix itself, and the reborn membership will cast a shadow of obscurity over those few who have made dangling the key today a sign of sham and hoax.

THE POWER
AND PITFALLS
OF THE
FOUNDATIONS

AMERICAN professors and universities dance to the tune of many pipers, but there are few they try to please more than the foundations. Foundation grants support conventional research and scholarship as well as all sorts of new efforts, many of which might otherwise conceivably languish. The prestige conferred upon professors and schools by foundation grants is generally worth many times the actual monetary award. Competition for foundation support is energetic and keen, and if the competition resulted in some discernibly significant improvement in creativity and scholarship commensurate with the time and money expended, one would have little to complain about. But the activity of foundations in recent years, in which they have reached a level of expenditure seemingly approaching that of the federal government itself, spending hundreds of millions and engaging the efforts of our leading academicians on projects of occasionally dubious value, raises the question whether their total influence on American higher education may not have been in some ways more harmful than helpful.

Of the 15,000 or so foundations in the United States dedicated to philanthropy, most are small, offering annual awards for their projects, not all of them in education, of from $2,000 to $5,000. About 150 foundations, however, have assets of at least $10,000,000, and these spend more than half of their grants on education. Seventy-five per cent of all foundation money comes from these 150. Of these giant establishments, the Ford Foundation is by far the most gigantic, giving away its money by the tens of millions: $25 million one year to the Fund for the Advancement of Education; $20 million to establish the National Merit Scholarships; $15 million to the Fund for the Republic; $21,500,000 to start the Woodrow Wilson National Fellowship Program, designed to increase the number of college teachers. In 1962 alone, the Ford Foundation gave more than $170 million to projects in education.

It takes no special acuity to see that foundations today profoundly affect the character of American education, whether they pour money by the millions into the treasuries of huge institutions, like Stanford or Harvard, or by the thousands into the private pockets of professors. It seems entirely safe to say that there is scarcely a faculty member or an administrator in the country who has not at least once considered applying for a foundation grant. No corner of a campus is so obscure as to have escaped the scrutiny of a foundation at some time, nor has any corner remained the same after such scrutiny. As Dwight Macdonald put it, perhaps excessively, "The American academic world, thanks partly to the foundations, is becoming a place where committees accumulate and thought decays."

Occasionally foundation directors recognize and express their awesome responsibility. Frederick T. Gates, adviser to John D. Rockefeller in his philanthropic endeavors, told a board meeting of the Rockefeller Foundation that when the members had to account for their work on earth to God, His only question to them would be: "What did you do as a trustee of the Rockefeller Foundation?" The Ford Foundation has been engaged since its founding in an almost continuous examination of its philanthropic policies. Yet in spite of all this acknowledged responsibility and self-appraisal, foundations as a group go on year after year perpetuating and solidifying questionable practices.

In an article in *The New York Times Magazine,* Waldemar A. Nielsen, president of the African-American Institute and a former executive of the Ford Foundation, summed up the shortcomings of foundation practice. One of his principal themes was that grants go to the "best investment," in terms of person and project. The professor or school with a proven record of "production" is more likely to get a new grant than anyone else; the project that fits the current fashion is favored over any path-breaking one. In addition, the foundations prefer obscure and highly generalized issues; these are likely to be "safer" and, at worst, will yield no results rather than unwelcome ones.

One obvious consequence has been overlapping and duplication. Recently, two foundations, their offices only a few blocks apart in New York City, were planning similar studies of higher education in Central America. An official of one even expressed concern that the other might "beat" it getting into the field. Just as schools compete with one another in applying for grants, the big foundations compete with one another in awarding them. Not only do the colleges and universities elbow one another aside as they wait for grants, the foundations themselves try to outdo one another in bestowing the money, often to the same people, sometimes for the same purposes. Competition may be healthy in driving down prices and raising quality in the open market; it's unlikely that competition lowers costs and improves research on campuses. For that matter, everyone will probably agree that competition which eliminates small operators in the academic community can only be bad.

Occasionally, in an attempt to drum up business, the foundations themselves will dream up projects and try to interest colleges and universities to undertake them. Or they will simply propose to offer an institution sums of money if someone will come up with a plausible project. I remember one man scurrying around an Eastern campus trying to get persons to suggest notions that might seem appropriate to a foundation that had indicated it had funds available. He came up with a project in "self-evaluation" (a favorite foundation word) of teaching on that campus, which eventually proved that he himself was so good a teacher that he could now become an administrator and leave the classroom forever (a distinct gain since he never had been much of a teacher anyway).

But even when there is little or no boondoggling, foundations can still work a pernicious effect. Only the most naive academician applies for a grant to Guggenheim, Ford, Rockefeller, or Carnegie simply on the basis of what he happens to think is important or needed. Applicants slant their projects on the basis of what they think the foundations will favor. Harold Laski succinctly sketched the dynamics of this process in describing the foundation executive. "He travels luxuriously," he wrote, "is amply entertained wherever he goes (he has so much to give), and he speaks always to hearers keenly alert to sense the direction of his own interests in order that they may explain that this is the one thing they are anxious to develop in their own university.... The foundations... have only to indicate the immediate direction of their minds for the whole university to discover that it always meant to gravitate swiftly to that angle of the intellectual compass."

Stringfellow Barr, himself the head of a foundation, one of the small ones, and a former college president, wrote a novel about academic life, *Purely Academic*. A foundation head is speaking: "Hungry, ambitious academics sit around, from coast to coast, cooking up 'projects' with an eye to pleasing the foundations. The projects all look as if they had been rewritten for style in some Federal bureau or other.... If you give them money—and you have to give some from time to time—that's what a philanthropoid is hired to do—they use it for some other ill-disguised purpose." Barr's description occurs in a fictional context, but every academic knows that many a tour in Europe has been financed by money granted for research in a library. Perhaps recognizing this tendency as a fact of life, or perhaps just trying to get rid of money with a minimum of decision-making, the Ford Foundation for a while simply and sensibly gave grants to professors just to take time off and do just about what they pleased, including traveling in Europe.

Many professors, of course, work only on the projects which they propose. But because these have probably been prepared with an eye to pleasing the foundations rather than the applicants themselves, they are not always likely to be the sort of free-searching, unslanted inquiries out of which the best results usually come. The sardonic suggestion has been made more than once that the Russians could probably do nothing better to tie up American scientific progress than to set up still another foundation with its own particular slant. Leo Szilard, the atomic physicist, speculated in a short story that the same end could be obtained by putting the best scientists on selection committees of foundations.

A friend of mine spoke somewhat bitterly about the issue; he had himself been the recipient of several grants. "If the foundations don't promote actual dishonesty," he said, "they encourage irrelevance. Some even grant the money for work past done, not for current or future work. The grant is in recognition of reputation. They serve like little Nobel prizes. This is fine when the foundation makes no bones about this, as in the recent ACLS awards to distinguished scholars in the humanities, $10,000 prizes for past achievement. But this is rarely done openly. If you have no reputation, any grant you get is a recognition of your ingenuity in thinking up a plausible enterprise." This is hyperbole, perhaps, but not by much. The Guggenheim Foundation, for example, originally established, as its statement of purpose says, to help persons in the arts and sciences under 40, donates a good deal of its money to those over 40, to persons with well established reputations.

As Nielsen points out, foundations take as few risks in bestowing their grants as they do in making their investments. Safest projects, for example, those guaranteed to offer some yield, however small, are surveys. Barr's foundation head comments: "Professors form research teams with small herds of secretaries, not to solve problems, but to study approaches to problems. More problems have been approached with foundation aid than you can imagine. It's an absolute miracle that one or two haven't been solved, if only by some untoward accident."

Foundations are subject to all the ills that bureaucracy is heir to: red tape; insecurity; unwillingness to take simple risks, let alone bold ones; a tendency to fall into comfortable grooves; a lack of concern which approaches indifference; cautiousness; and so on. To avoid mistakes, foundations sometimes look as if they make only mistakes. For all of their huge apparatus of decision and selection, the foundations probably cannot prove that they can do as well as a lottery. Individual philanthropy, in spite of its occasional whimsy, as Macdonald wrote, citing Maecenas and "the rich American lady who helped support Joyce while he was writing *Ulysses,* has a record of success at least as impressive as that of the university and foundation committees of our day, including the one that gives out Guggenheim Fellowships." As in any bureaucracy, as Macdonald puts it, "there is a tendency toward the mediocre, the mean level of the board or committee that is making the decision." When Lady Luck operates alone, the odds that a good award will be made (once minimal qualifications are met) are at least as good as those that a poor one will be.

Nielsen's comment is pertinent here. "Very few foundation projects have turned out to be complete failures—a fact which is in itself disquieting, because one suspects that there would have been more failures if the approach to grant-making had been more daring. This is the nub of the issue and the real source of concern: the high proportion of mediocre grants."

Foundations as they presently operate simply cannot be depended on for seeking out imaginative, significant possibilities on their own. Their personnel are likely to be constantly moving about. An assignment as a philanthropoid is often considered second-best to a good academic appointment, however much the foundations pay. The foundation director in Barr's novel is entirely cynical about his work; he hires a professor to be his assistant by offering to provide a sybaritic interlude. When foundations do try to be original, they are likely to emerge with bizarre or whimsical projects. No wonder that foundations follow the rule that the better part of philanthropy is conventionality.

Like any bureaucracy anxious about serving its clientele but confused about how best to do so, foundations sabotage themselves. For all of their eagerness to give away money to deserving causes, they often make the task of applying for a grant a Herculean effort. "I want to finish a novel," a friend of mine, a much published writer, said to me, "but I think it would be just as easy to write it as to ask for a grant to subsidize me. What I need is a fellowship to support me while I fill out the application."

The annual appeal for foundation funds affects the entire academic community. If persons are not themselves filling out applications forms, they are writing letters of recommendation. "One year," a professor said, "I couldn't get around to my own request for a grant because I was so busy writing letters for friends and students." The writing of lavish and excessive letters of praise has been brought to a high level of hyperbole, for professors have long ago learned that a straightforward appraisal will scarcely be visible to a philanthropoid used to reading flamboyant descriptions of the heroes and giants described in competing letters.

Fashions in philanthropy are often established without relation to need or to the character of a discipline. In the social sciences, for example, foundation emphasis has been on the "hard," scientific approach, the gathering of objective data, and the working together of social scientists in teams. As Macdonald and William H. Whyte, Jr., have pointed out, this has resulted in the neglect of the "lone" worker, the man who by himself can work out an important theory or concept, men like Marx, Weber, Freud, Whyte himself. It is perhaps not excessive to suggest that this foundation emphasis has done more than any other one factor to change the direction of social science today. Whether this is good or bad is not to the point here so much as the fact that an academic discipline has been profoundly affected by a foundation philosophy, itself the result of administrative exigencies. "It takes more careful study, more careful investigation to make a grant of $5,000 to one individual," Charles Dollard, then head of the Carnegie Corporation, told a Congressional committee, "than it does to give a grant of a half million to a well-established university...."

Whyte bears down on this particular aspect of foundation

giving. "In making grants, [the foundations] channel the bulk of their money to large-scale team projects and programs.... Academics joke privately (and bitterly) that it's easier to get $500,000 from a foundation than $5,000; understandably many react by inflating their projects, and the more they do so, the more satisfied the foundations are that their way of giving is the proper way."

A favorite way for foundations to distribute money is to give it in million-dollar chunks to established schools provided the schools raise equal sums. "All this does," a university administrator pointed out to me, "is simply enable a particular school to become even more like itself than it was before. If the school was pretty good to begin with, it will continue to be good. If it was mediocre, mediocrity is expanded. It's unlikely that money alone will change the character of a university. With all of the millions the Ford Foundation has poured into university treasuries with practically no strings attached, it could easily have started a new and undoubtedly first-rate school in a section of the country that desperately needed one and is not likely to get it through public sources."

It is certainly true that the backing of going concerns has not served to encourage experimentation or pioneering. The boldest recent proposal in higher education, for example, the plan by the University of California to establish a complex of diversified small colleges at Santa Cruz, is supported by public funds. It is ironic that foundations, originally set up to promote originality and to take risks in behalf of discovery, have settled down, like staid legislatures, to the disbursement of funds to established, traditional enterprises. It remains for an enlightened public body to envision and plan a truly new sort of academic community.

Barr's foundation head related the problems of foundations to the total social scene: "There's not much a founda-

76

tion can do. Broadly speaking, it has even more means at its disposal than a university has. But it has an equally ill-defined end. In short, it's a microcosm of our society: abundant means but no ends. You know: the American way of life, as they call it."

The foundations do indeed often seem to operate with a peculiarly American profligacy and with a damn-the-public kind of independence in spite of all current attempts to make it appear that only the best interests of the public are being served. We may find justification for lavishness, even for a certain amount of waste, in business life, especially when a firm shows a profit and there's no question about the nature of the profit. The Ford Motor Company may comfortably if not happily throw down the drain tens of millions of dollars in developing the Edsel; over-all, the company remains productive and may even plausibly write up the experience gained from the Edsel as worth the loss. There is less justification, if any, for the Ford Foundation to sink millions into pointless projects or into some, like its work with adult education, which another foundation, Carnegie, had already established as a dubious investment. It is one thing for the Ford Motor Company to keep its plans for new models hidden from General Motors, but there is no equally apparent reason for the Ford Foundation to keep its projects secret from the Carnegie or Rockefeller foundations, or for all three to come out with identical projects like so many competing models.

Foundations today follow their own consciences, which, it is true, are highly sensitive instruments. But these consciences are still in fact limited to their boards of directors. In spite of the occasional outcries of conservative Congressmen, however, few foundation activities are ever consciously opposed to the public welfare. But to say that they don't oppose the best interests of the public is not to say that they

77

always serve them. While it may seem beyond question good to devote $50 million to raising faculty salaries throughout the country, it may not have been good beyond question to establish the Fund for the Republic, to cite only one particular, much criticized foundation enterprise. And there is nothing to prevent a wealthy and bigoted oil millionaire, say, from setting up a foundation to support colleges and universities which will exclude Jews, Catholics, and Negroes, among others; indeed such attempts have been made. There is nothing to prevent foundations from following any whimsy in making grants, from pursuing will-o'-the-wisps in science and scholarship, even from supporting enterprises which may have obvious short-term benefits but hidden long-term dangers (like lavishing money on big schools to the ultimate end that small ones may be forced altogether out of the competitive academic market).

Dwight Macdonald, in his brilliant and doubtlessly definitive study of the Ford Foundation [1] (which in its own form should serve as a model to foundations of what a study should really be), suggested that most foundation problems stem from their impersonal, bureaucratic set-up. "The dilemma confronting the philanthropoid," he wrote, "is that of King Midas—his golden touch robs everything of its natural qualities." He points out that while an individual may give away his money with an abandon that no one would challenge, the most carefully considered gift of a foundation is immediately challenged. "This, among other things," he remarked, "explains the timidity of the great foundations in the face of criticism from the public, the press, and Congress—they are almost as public-relations conscious as the great corporations—and also their reluctance to go very far in encouraging the new and untried."

[1] The quotations of Whyte, Dollard, and Laski here are taken from Macdonald's study.

78

Perhaps precisely because they have to walk the thin line between protecting their private freedom and demonstrating their social responsibility, the possibilities for mischief and waste are multiplied. Several paradoxes and ironies operate. Some persons, like conservative Congressmen, who are likely to insist that it is good and proper for foundations to remain private, competitive corporations, are likely also to complain that the foundations sponsor causes that are daring or radical. Liberal spokesmen are likely to complain about the conservative nature of foundation policy and advocate government supervision. It is safer for foundations almost to risk much waste than to risk too great success. Waste, especially when spread out, is less visible than success.

The establishment of some central agency simply to help eliminate duplication, overlapping, repetition of projects, however, as Nielsen suggests, might work some reforms without drastically changing the character and operation of foundations. A good argument may be made out that the government itself has every right to establish such a supervising agency since the Ford Foundation was created, among other reasons, to save some 300 million dollars in inheritance taxes; surely this alone would seem to give the people some right to examine the expenditure of moneys which might otherwise have gone into the public treasury. But, of course, the proposed agency might simply be an arm of the several large foundations, and it might indeed be preferable to keep it free from any additional paralysis of thought and action which might be contributed by federal bureaucracy.

This agency would neither control nor necessarily advise, but would merely inform. Foundations have functioned long enough by now to have scored a number of unmistakable successes and failures, to have considered all sorts of possible projects which were rejected for good reason after careful analysis and deliberation. The results of past work would be made widely known so that the same infertile field need not be plowed again and again, at least without knowledge aforethought.

Positively, such an agency could lay out areas of concern in which foundations might profitably operate. Philanthropy need not be haphazard. As it is, some of the foundations already specialize. Rockefeller supports science; Ford, international amity; Guggenheim, the arts and scholarship. What is needed is an understanding among them as to their primary responsibilities. As their orientations narrow, the wisdom and the efficiency with which their grants are distributed should increase.

The agency might serve as a self-policing body as well, informing particular foundations when their grants seemed to be departing too widely from their stated purposes, advising all of them that certain areas in our national life are being neglected. For years, foundations have been favoring the physical and social sciences to the neglect of the arts. Happily, the Ford Foundation recently announced that it will seek to correct this imbalance and find ways of supporting creative effort more substantially. "An Office of Foundation Study" might have helped some foundation see this need earlier and see its dimensions and its character as well.

An independent agency could objectively and wisely advise the expenditure of great sums to set up subsidiary funds, like the Fund for the Republic (which, as Macdonald pointed out, has been described by cynics as the severance pay for a number of Ford Foundation executives), or to sponsor the founding of new colleges or the elaborate expansion of existing ones. The agency would also be in the best position to study the relation between foundation and government practice. As Nielsen put it, "More open channels of communication between foundations and government could give the former a clearer focus on problems which, from a broad national point of view, require attention. Top-level consultation could also identify overlaps and gaps between foundations and government and thereby bring about better allocation of available resources—without subjecting the foundations to official coordination."

While such an office might help the foundations with project grants, those involving groups of persons, it is not likely to help much in improving the distribution of funds to individual scholars, scientists, artists. It may be advisable for the foundations to consider putting this distribution more directly into the hands of those already responsible professionally for the evaluation of art and the dissemination of knowledge: museum and gallery directors; gallery heads; orchestra conductors; magazine editors; reputable publishers, both commercial and university; department chairmen, college deans, and other university administrators; private laboratory heads; library directors. These persons know intimately the working young scholars, painters, composers, writers. They can more nearly function like Maecenas. Editors of quality magazines, for instance, would be enabled to pay better fees. The Ford Foundation had one project of supporting university press publication of books by faculty members whose institutions had no press. The director and the editor of the publishing press, and not persons at the foundations, however, determined what should be published. A faculty member's superior should be better able to tell whether he can produce a meaningful piece of work than a committee judging him and his project on the basis of letters of recommendation. A commercial publisher with foundation money would more readily take on noncommercial but worthy books and would simultaneously be exercising his professional judgment about the capacity of the persons actually to produce these books. Certainly an

81

arrangement like this would be subject to abuse, but to no more than the present system. While some such arrangements have been established here and there, they have been short-lived and niggardly.

A direct source from which we might expect some help in solving the problems surrounding foundations is the government itself. For all of the money given by the foundations, more projects are turned down than are approved. The government might use its resources to redress imbalances, to step into areas where foundations have hesitated to tread. The pattern of government spending on medical and scientific research has been much influenced by the Rockefeller Foundation, and the government has been increasing its aid in these areas until it now far surpasses anything any foundation can do. Conceivably, the process might be reversed, government patterns might influence foundations, either by breaking paths, setting up precedents and procedures, or simply by taking over some of the areas now the province of foundations, thus leaving them free to experiment and pioneer.

For all of their influence on American higher education, however, it seems to me a question finally whether foundations can really change the fundamental character of a university or of a particular discipline, let alone that of the whole landscape. (It is too early, of course, to tell whether the massive efforts of the Ford Foundation to make educational television a potent force have had any real effect.) Individual path-breaking in the social sciences still goes on; young persons of talent, ambition, and energy still make their way without Guggenheims; bold, vast experiments in education still take place without Ford.

Certainly, the effort in the early part of the century to change the quality of American medical education was immensely successful, but how can one say that the improvement of the medical schools might not have been spontaneously generated anyway, in different ways, of course, at different rates, for different reasons. Important needs make themselves felt, one way or another.

Consider faculty salaries. Perhaps the Ford Foundation has contributed observably to the country-wide improvement of salaries through its disbursement of $50 million; that much money would certainly seem to be enough to cause more than a ripple, even in the academic ocean. But salaries have been going up slowly and steadily, affected by such things as the general rise in the cost of living, the competition with private industry for faculty personnel, the increasing pressure for everyone to get a college education. Salaries today, it is not outlandish to speculate, might not be very much lower without that $50 million.

Nor can one long sustain a reasonable complaint, I think, that necessary work on campuses which foundations have not supported has indeed languished. Scholars and scientists of any worth, with any serious dedication to their subjects, usually generate enough momentum on their own to find their own ways and means of doing their work whether or not the foundations come through with support. (Indeed, some such persons will not bother to take the time off to fill out the interminable applications.) Some of the best scholarly and creative work in this country has been done without a penny's aid from the foundations. It may seem unjust from some perspective that fashionable but worthless projects are supported lavishly, but this is one of the lesser inequities serious academicians learn to shrug away.

Some institutions have become grant-happy, hiring persons experienced in the ways of soliciting aid, devoting whole offices to funneling funds onto the campus. It is not likely that in the absence of a sense of quality, a tradition of scholarship, a dedicated faculty, these places can much

83

improve; indeed, some of the evidence suggests the contrary: some institutions which have devoted themselves single-mindedly to getting foundation help have neglected the essential functions of a university and have clearly slipped: administrators proliferate and faculty dissipates. Certainly Harvard's stature, to cite a reverse instance, has not diminished by a millimetre because of its refusal to accept federal funds for classified research, funds which many other schools have used to try to improve the whole campus.

There are only so many good schools, so many good men, so many good students, so many meaningful projects, and all of the money in the world will neither increase their number nor corrupt all of them. Certainly foundations can work much good in the academic community, and many have already done much good, however expensively and accidentally, but it is not likely that the harm they can do will really outweigh the good. Academic mendicants and malingerers and joy-riders have always been with us, and if they were not being supported by foundations, they'd be sponging on their fellows. Foolish and pointless work has always been done and will always be done, with or without foundations; and so will good work.

Surely some things might be done to improve the operation of the foundations simply because waste, inefficiency, mischief in the academic landscape, any warping of the academic structure, are all undesirable. But nothing should be done in panic or in anger or in cynicism. Perhaps the greatest harm the foundations have done is almost to persuade us and themselves that our colleges and universities, our intellectual life in general, can no longer function so well without them. Certainly the academic world must continue to be properly grateful for foundation aid, but it must also develop ways of determining the widespread and long-

84

term effects of this aid. We can never expect either individuals or institutions to reject gifts casually, but if the foundations themselves do not develop wiser ways of giving, then simply out of self-protection the individuals and institutions will have to develop wiser ways of asking and of taking. It may be better to learn to do without altogether than to have to learn to live with an embarrassment of riches. American higher education, which has learned to accept various sorts of violent shocks, will one way or another learn to absorb the shock of the foundations.

BREAKING
THE PH.D.
BARRIER

*"...for every 10 college teachers now employed, some-
where between 16 and 25 new ones will have to be found
between now and 1970."* Teachers for Tomorrow (Fund
for the Advancement of Education, New York, 1955),
p. 19.

IN SPITE OF the pressing and uni-
versally acknowledged need for more college and university
teachers in every discipline, it remains almost as difficult
as ever to enter the academic landscape confidently. The
main obstacle, of course, is becoming a Doctor of Philosophy. The degree is often cynically called "the union card."
Without the degree, one is practically naked in that landscape, subject to all of the harsh changes of the climate.

It is possible to teach in some junior and teachers colleges
with only a master's degree, sometimes with only a bachelor's, and some persons who have made reputations for
themselves by producing work that has been, somewhat
smugly, described as "the equivalent of a doctorate" may
get regular appointments at major colleges and universities
without a Ph.D. (this is especially true of Britons). But to
obtain tenure, to be promoted, usually just to establish oneself on a respectable basis, the Ph.D. is virtually indispensable for an American.

This would seem eminently reasonable. The physician is expected to have his medical degree, the lawyer his law degree. The Ph.D. is the professional degree for the college teacher. Unfortunately the matter is not that simple. At its worst, the Ph.D. obstacle course can be described as an elimination contest, designed not to prepare anyone for college teaching but to discourage everyone from it. And even at its best, the work for the Ph.D. might be described as irrelevant to the duties the college teacher is expected to perform.

The statistics are indeed dismal. The number of years necessary to get the doctorate in the arts, social sciences, or sciences at Columbia University, for example, used to exceed the time put in by physicians and lawyers before they begin their practice. From 1940 to 1956, about 60 of the 225 students enrolled in English and Comparative Literature spent from eight to nine years on their doctorates. About 15 had been at the work for 20 years or more! In mathematics, one quarter of the students had spent 8 to 9 years; in history, 32 per cent took 6 to 7 years; in physics, 37 per cent took the same time. No doctorate in the Faculties of Political Science, Philosophy, or Pure Science took fewer than five years.

Of course, much can be done, sometimes by mere administrative tightening, to decrease the prolongation of the preparation. Most doctoral students, for example, do not pursue their studies full-time; stipends of various sorts have already begun to help a few of them. In some schools, no limitation is put on the number of years students may devote to the degree; the cancelling of credit for courses done, say, five or more years before work for the degree is completed is keeping students from stretching out their work indefinitely. New faculty members, too, have become aware of the realities and are urging and aiding students to get their work done in sensible time. At the great graduate

87

schools, the story is that there always used to be at least one professor whose motto was "Grow old along with me."

But the very nature of the degree, at least as it is at present conceived of, will always keep it from being, like the M.D. or the B.LL., subject to a neat curriculum. For one thing, there just can be no efficient, fixed arrangement of courses for all Ph.D.'s in all disciplines. The sociology student will need statistics, say; the English specialist will have to study Old English; the French student, Old French. Courses in one discipline are likely to require different periods of preparation from those in another. But more important than differences in course work, and differences in language requirements, are the differences in dissertation subjects. For the Ph.D. is not, like the M.D. and the law degree, a "vocational" degree, one preparing its holder for a profession. It is a research degree, first and last. It is not uncommon to find a student devoting more time to writing his thesis than he did to all of his previous schooling, including his doctoral course work.

But, again, even the time and work exacted to write the dissertation are not so much the problem as the nature of the work. In actual fact, true research is often discouraged. The attitude of most faculty is that little new remains to be done; the student who is intensely involved in his field, straining to find or to say something original, is often squelched. "To most graduates the choice of the topic for the dissertation is difficult," writes Professor G. B. Harrison, "because they lack a sense of direction and reality. The best topics have long since been mined; there remain only the slag heaps of former explorers. The few who aspire to become scholars are often prematurely ambitious. . . . For this reason, when asked by a puzzled graduate to suggest topics for his dissertation, I usually advise him to consider editing a text." And the professor might have added that

88

the more obscure the text the better; its literary quality should as much as possible be kept irrelevant. No wonder students who enter graduate work as a labor of love often leave it in frustration and hatred.

It is this sort of narrowness and cynicism which impelled the brilliant but bitter analysis of the graduate student's lot by Theodore Solotaroff in *Commentary*.

> In terms of his intellectual development, the peculiar circumstances of the graduate student's private life foster the process by which even the intellectually ambitious and independent student eventually fits himself into the mold of the efficient, unobjectionable young scholar. The daily price that not only he but his wife (and children) are paying for him to remain in school impels him to steer a prudential course. The man who is struggling to keep his head above water is not likely to try diving for pearls. The student may even come to prefer the routine but manageable course to the challenging but difficult one; the low-pressured, humane, sensible professor to the brilliant but unreliable man; the trivial but safe dissertation topic to the adventurous and problematic one. He learns to go along with the acceptable style of scholarly thinking, in which "originality" means mainly finding a problem, or segment of one, that is still to be explored, "pertinence" means mainly the amount of fresh factual documentation that can be accumulated, and "soundness" means mainly working within the existing body of "scholarly opinion."

Solotaroff, himself a former graduate student at the University of Chicago, concedes the value of the discipline involved in writing the dissertation. The graduate student, he says, "realizes that competent scholarship does temper the mind, that to suspend value judgments can contribute to understanding, that small discoveries have their own excitement." Nevertheless, the overwhelming testimony, Solotaroff concludes, points to the stultifying effect of most graduate work. One graduate professor summed up this attitude: "Before I graduated from Harvard with my Ph.D., I was a human being. After, I became an academic machine."

No doubt there is a great gap between one's first impulse to study literature, history, psychology, anthropology, chemistry and the final effort required to teach the subject. The high school or college student excited about reading Shakespeare or Eliot or Kafka discovers that he has to learn the history of the English language before he can teach literature in college; the psychology student discovers that he must know a good deal of statistics before he can teach Freud.

But education in general often seems like a simple series of disenchantments. I remember my own career. In high school, we talked about texts: *Macbeth,* Dostoyevsky, Dickinson, Millay. I was aroused and excited. In college, we began on dates, on lists of "influences," on "periods." In graduate school, we concentrated on what the critics and scholars had said; it seemed almost more important to know Kittredge's classification of the *Canterbury Tales* than to have read them and responded to the text. How does one keep one's momentum of commitment alive? The subject itself fades into the distance; the apparatus for approaching it is mastered; but one is not allowed to get too near. Solotaroff summed up the changes in the new Ph.D.

> He has become more narrow, diligent, and cautious in his ideas, more respectable in his style of thinking and writing, more politic in his behavior. He worries more about being "sound" than being stimulating; he finds it more natural to adopt a middle position rather than an extreme one, an academically fashionable stance rather than a personal one. He is likely to be more in touch with "scholarly opinion" about his subject than with his own feelings, intuitions, and

sense of relevance, and thus to find himself having as much difficulty thinking and writing about history or literature or politics or society in direct, open, non-technical terms as he once had in disciplining his personal demands on his field to the methods and vocabulary of research. The gain in his ability to contribute to the learned journals can involve the loss of the intellectual energy or confidence to communicate beyond them. Five or six years is a long time. The graduate student who once cynically put on the mask of the conventional scholar, planning in his heart to remove it as soon as he had his degree, finds often enough that his face—as George Orwell remarked in another connection—has grown to fit it.

Or so it can seem. But everywhere is the sensitive and intelligent teacher, always ready himself to be taught, always ready to engage a student who has an original but valid response (originality without content is all too common and is the bane of any teacher). The alert and serious student seeks out the "good" teachers, avoids the "bad" ones. He learns a new terrain of study; he sees his field not differently but in a new perspective. Freud by way of statistics has a new significance; Milton through Spenser and through prosody is a larger Milton.

All of the dangers to the free, broadly ranging, unhampered intellectual life that Solotaroff catalogues are actual but beside the point. They exist everywhere: in publishing, in advertising, in Hollywood, in Washington, in research laboratories, in libraries, in law offices. One makes his way around them, especially if one can recognize them. They are part of the landscape. As well complain of the thistle or the rut in the field, the cow dung or the skunk odor, and close oneself off to sky and mountain and forest and lake. Some of the finest intellectual activity in the United States has been carried out in the graduate schools, in the course of completing doctoral requirements. (I think of Krutch's work on Restoration comedy; Barzun's on 19th century intellectual history; Handlin's on American immigration; Trilling's on Matthew Arnold.)

But to say that productive work can be done while getting the doctorate is not to say that it is done as a result of the particular requirements of the degree; more often it is done in spite of them. To say that we can avoid pitfalls is not to say that they should be there. I happen to think that most of the requirements for the doctorate make sense, but I also happen to think that many of them can easily be taken care of at earlier stages of one's education and in other ways than are conventional at present. There is no reason why language requirements, for example, in French, German, and even Latin, the usual ones for most degrees, cannot be met in the course of work for the bachelor's degree. (Of course, many students simply pursue the curriculum of their undergraduate colleges, most of which have been gradually relaxing the requirements to take foreign languages. It is up to the student seriously interested in a career of college teaching to take care of these essential but fringe needs early.) Also, a good undergraduate preparation in a subject should enable a student to devote himself to truly becoming a specialist while working for his doctorate. Taking courses in graduate school to make up "deficiencies" in preparation is clearly wasteful.

Most graduate schools follow a system of virtually triplicating the examination of every student: he is examined and graded in each course, he goes through what is called a "preliminary" or a "qualifying" oral examination, and finally he takes written "comprehensives" which often last as long as a forty-hour week. This system is nothing less than triple jeopardy. Surely at least two of these measurements can be dispensed with or considerably relaxed. At

Columbia's graduate school, in English, a student goes through only the oral examination, which, of course, can be traumatic for many persons since so much depends on a two-hour performance. But at least the trauma comes only once.

Other reforms to make the doctoral system more humane and more efficient will surely suggest themselves to any professors, administrators, and students genuinely concerned about changing the nature of the preparation from an elimination course to one introducing the student to college teaching. These will differ from institution to institution, of course, for there is a minimum of uniformity to be found from one graduate school to another. I do not think that any of these changes should in any way adulterate the essence, the character, of the degree, which, whatever else it may be and however it may be derided, seems to me still to mark the indispensable professional preparation for college teaching.

The primacy of the Ph.D. degree seems to be conceded even by those involved in finding short-cuts and substitutes for it. For example, the Fund for the Advancement of Education, a Ford Foundation enterprise, is sponsoring at several universities throughout the country what is described as a three-year master's program leading to college teaching. Under this plan, the student starts his preparation in the junior year of his undergraduate career, specifically enrolling in courses related to college teaching. He is expected by the time he finishes his graduate year to have concluded work in two languages as well as enough work in his major field, including his master's essay, to begin teaching his subject in college, at least on the freshman and sophomore levels. The program calls for stipends for the students, beginning in the first year and increasing each year until in the third year it is equivalent to that earned by a teaching assistant, who is usually someone who already has the M.A. and is working toward the doctorate. The student in the program is supposed to work closely with senior professors on tasks introducing him to the details of college teaching; in his last year, he takes over teaching duties under the supervision of his mentor.

One of the acknowledged problems in this program is that it might set up two classes of "citizenship" among college faculty, those with only the M.A. and those with the Ph.D. While this may eventually have to occur anyway, simply because of the coming shortage of Ph.D.'s for college teaching, it is not considered at the moment a happy situation. Indeed, it is hoped that the M.A.'s trained under this program will have gone so far toward the doctorate that they will find it a simple matter to go the extra distance on their own. Certainly the program holds promise for filling the ranks of college teachers, at the lower levels anyway, with properly trained persons who may indeed not wish to pursue graduate education any farther than the M.A. (like wives of faculty members).

The Ph.D. remains the *sine qua non* for college teaching in America. But there is certainly nothing inviolable or sacrosanct about the procedures necessary to obtain it. Not only might the degree itself be made a more sensible and more efficient one to obtain, but its content might be so modified as to revitalize its traditional character: a degree evidencing a person's mastery of a field in general, his having become singly expert on some specific aspect of it, and his having proved himself prepared to teach on the college level both the general and the specific areas to others.

Certainly, too, there is no point in maintaining the image of the Ph.D. candidate as the American equivalent of the starving painter or writer on the Left Bank in Paris. One graduate professor in an Eastern school used to say that no graduate student really knew what it meant to become a college teacher until he had to live on bread and cheese for weeks and light his apartment with candles. It is likely that the increasing availability of stipends for all kinds of graduate work will by itself help change this image. And if the program can be made tighter and neater and more nearly continuous, lasting not more than, say, a medical student's total training, some five or six years after the baccalaureate, then Ph.D. candidates might find themselves leading more or less normal lives more nearly comparable with those of law or medical students, or even of junior executives of equivalent age.

Nor does there seem to be any need to maintain the Germanic character of the doctorate. Not only might the course work be arranged to accord more nearly with reality (it simply is fantasy to expect that anyone can become encyclopedically expert in any of the usual disciplines today), but the dissertation subject itself might be appropriately modified to be a meaningful but not necessarily exhaustive study of a particular subject. It used to be that all dissertations had to be published, leading in many instances to an additional enormous expense for the student who could not find a publisher. Vanity publishing for a while flourished. But publication is not necessarily a meaningless expectation, and, indeed, publication of graduate research is now beginning to occur again but much more relevantly. Some institutions have been asking that students make their master's essay the equivalent—in content and form—of a contribution to one of the learned journals in the student's field. Some schools have been encouraging a doctoral study that is not simply a piece of pedantic scholarship but also a critical contribution. Some of the studies have consisted of several discrete essays on one subject or on one figure. Many of these have been of sufficiently high quality to warrant almost immediate publication. I have in mind recent books issued by the university presses at California, Cornell, Columbia, Harvard.

The work done by the doctoral candidate to earn whatever stipend happens to be available on his campus ought to be more significantly integrated with his study and research. It is false economy for the entire university community to use doctoral candidates only as cheap labor for introductory courses, as is all too common. The candidates do themselves little good, for often their teaching is only remotely related to their competency or their study; their undergraduate students lose much. But certainly every field calls for research and scholarship which a doctoral candidate can do profitably, furthering his own study, helping a senior professor. When the candidate is assigned classroom duties, these might well occasionally be in more advanced areas rather than in introductory ones only. In short, that gap between the candidate's work for his stipend and his work for his degree ought to be narrowed and, hopefully, altogether closed.

Finally, it ought to be acknowledged once and for all that doctoral candidates are not preparing themselves only or mainly for careers in libraries or laboratories. They will be college teachers. Apprentice or intern arrangements are surely one way to orient them for their careers in the classrooms. All too often the beginning teacher is thrust into a classroom to make his own way, no one either advising him or supervising him. He learns the problems of teaching his specialty entirely by hit or miss. In a sense this trial and error method duplicates some of the approaches in his research and will afford some extremely valuable learning, but it might easily and properly be supplemented by some sort of discussion or study. Everyone can use the experience of others, one way or another, if sometimes only to reject it.

Colleges protest too much that there is nothing to teaching. But surely there is a point between neglecting the problem altogether as though it actually had no existence and requiring college teachers to take courses in "methods of teaching freshman sociology," which would no doubt please the professional educationists and horrify the professional scholars. All that may be necessary is a more or less informal gathering of beginning instructors with experienced ones to discuss some of the problems, approaches, techniques of teaching in a particular field. It is even conceivable that the older professors might learn from their younger colleagues; there are few substitutes for eagerness, vitality, freshness.

The lot of the American graduate student is certainly not a happy one. But it does little good, I think, to become sentimentally bitter about it. Little more is wrong with the life of the graduate student than is wrong with any other single aspect of American higher education. Which is to say perhaps very little, for it would not be difficult to find that everything is rotten in academia. But improvements are obviously taking place, sometimes directed consciously and intelligently, sometimes arising out of the mere force of circumstances. Higher education, fortunately, can no longer be neglected.

Perhaps the primary responsibility for improving the graduate student's lot does indeed rest on the academic community itself. We should quite reasonably expect to see that community improve matters on all fronts: stipends, course work, examinations, dissertation subjects, publication, training for teaching, placing of students in jobs, and so on. Some of this, as I have indicated, is being done. Much of what is not being done is being at least discussed; in some places it is actually being planned for.

But some responsibility, I think, rests on the graduate student himself. Too many graduate students simply fall apart under the loose discipline of graduate schools. It is true that, as Jacques Barzun once said, many graduate students seem to need geriatric counseling, but even when they do not reach this stage, many seem incapable of making their own schedules of deadlines, integrating their course work with their research or teaching (when such opportunity presents itself), in short, of accepting the different pace and rhythm of graduate work. In graduate school, perhaps for the first time in his career, the American student becomes his own master, and the self-discipline and responsibility called for in this new role are sometimes too much for him to handle comfortably.

The case histories of graduate students who take decades to complete their doctoral work, who drift away into all sorts of other work, who go through the agonies of beginning families while oppressed financially and academically, are all too common and all too harrowing to be dismissed. But the less sensational case histories also exist, of students who plan their course work to be completed within a certain period, more or less; who plan their dissertation subjects sensibly and realistically, taking into account not only their enthusiasms and capabilities but the limitations of the subject itself; who get married and have children but recognize the necessary restrictions and guide themselves accordingly. (The problem of the young man in his twenties torn between beginning a career in the world and a life with a family is not by any means limited to the academic landscape. Young businessmen, physicians, lawyers, editors, writers, engineers, advertising copy-writers—all have similar problems.)

The one real disadvantage to the doctoral rites of passage is that often the academic landscape becomes distorted. Either it is seen as an Eden-like refuge, or it becomes a corner of Hell. It can, of course, approach both states. The doctoral candidate must be careful not to be misled by mirages; that is not El Dorado on the horizon, nor is it Hades. It is a place simply to practice a particular way of life, some of whose pleasures and satisfactions are clear enough to the candidate, for he has made his commitment. Faith and dedication are old-fashioned virtues and sometimes irrelevant, but entering into the career of professor— a career which has in itself at least two main divisions: that of preparation and that of actual practice—requires at least these two qualities: faith that one's choice is indeed a good one, whatever disillusionments rise along the way; dedication to getting through the passage, anesthetized to the harrassments which, hopefully, will indeed diminish and disappear once the ritual is concluded.

THE
SLAVE MARKET
AND THE
SLAVES

ONE OF the more dismal chores of an academic career is getting one's first regular job, Ph.D. in hand. Like so many other arrangements in American higher education, there is little system or logic to the process, and what may hold true in one discipline or area will not hold true in another, what may be the pattern at one time will not be the pattern at another. Occasionally, one of the major professional organizations in a discipline will attempt to impose some order on the anarchy, but all sorts of different and private arrangements continue to flourish alongside, some indeed even developing as a kind of reaction to, the new system. The flexibility and chaos are perhaps desirable in and of themselves, for they testify to a reluctance on the part of both administrators and candidates to be regimented; they also allow for a freedom of action that can favor originality. But the anarchy puts an unfairly heavy burden on the candidate to make his own way, which may also be a good thing, except that the intricacies of getting a decent academic appointment are utterly unrelated to the skills necessary for getting the doctorate, and perhaps even farther removed from those necessary to perform competently as a professor.

Perhaps the greatest obstacle the new Ph.D. faces in job

hunting is his own attitude toward selling himself. After all, he is likely to have decided on an academic career in the first place at least partly because of the refuge a campus seems to offer from the uncomfortable competitive struggles of the industrial and commercial worlds. The candidate for an academic job has spent the last several years quite removed from the irritations and exigencies of daily life; a fellowship or an assistantship has provided, however barely, for minimal needs; his occupation and preoccupation have been with his subject matter. Suddenly he has to push all this in the background and put to work whatever talents he can muster of the salesman or huckster. It is no wonder that many naive candidates take what seems to be the most comfortable and efficient way for finding a job, registering with an agency, a way which can also be one of the surest routes into the graves of academe.

It is not the least anomaly of academic job-hunting that agencies, which should be an obvious way of centralizing and rationalizing the whole process, are used almost not at all by most public and private institutions that hold a certain image of themselves (hard to define except in negative terms) or by Ph.D.'s who want jobs at these places. Agencies serve almost exclusively small denominational colleges in out-of-the-way locations, teachers' colleges, some state aggie colleges, junior colleges. It is next to impossible to move "up" from one of these institutions to a known state university or private college; they constitute an almost separate academic world (often justly so: longer hours, lower pay, poorer students, inadequate libraries, restrictions on personal habits and independent classroom performance, etc.). I know several instances of persons with good degrees who took the agency route and now simply cannot get out of this world of academic untouchables; the schools they would like to go to will have nothing to do with someone

101

who has "stooped" to take these jobs, however good the candidate's publication or teaching record: there must have been something "wrong" with him in the first place to have to take a job through an agency.

And, of course, there is usually something "wrong" with candidates who do not know enough not to commit academic suicide by registering with an agency. What is "wrong" is simply the candidate's naivete about this particular academic reality, or perhaps his firm refusal to take an active part in publicizing himself. In an attempt to change this image of themselves, some agencies seem to have taken to representing the institution in finding persons for jobs, that is, the candidate himself does not have to register, he is simply approached by the agency acting in behalf of an institution. This is a relatively new development, and it might well be a healthy one if it can do the task properly of matching school and candidate with a minimum expenditure of administration and faculty time and effort.

But the continuing chaos in placement and the failure of the agencies to achieve respectability testify to the importance put on personal contact, face-to-face interviewing, the use of the grapevine by administrators to find out about likely candidates, and its use by the candidates to find out about likely jobs. In short, no one seems really to want to rationalize the system, for then whim and luck and instinct and taste will no longer operate to the extent they do, and these, after all, make college teaching the kind of highly independent enterprise it is. It is perhaps in this area of American higher education alone that some degree of the subjective and the whimsical might profitably be preserved.

Theoretically it would seem that all institutions operate on the same principle in hiring faculty, that of getting the best person for a particular opening. Obviously, who is "best" is subject to a wide range of judgment. But a number of clearly irrelevant standards often apply as well, subject to no very rational control. Many departments, for example, will not hire one of their own graduates, however good he may be, until he proves himself elsewhere, that is, obtains a reputation off his own campus, and some will not even hire him then. This taboo against inbreeding, often applied with the same irrational rigidity that governs taboos in a primitive society, may well have at its basis the obvious explanation that departments observing it are uncertain of their own quality; they do not trust their graduates to be as good as those from other departments. To an extent this is true, obviously, even if it is put in altogether different terms, that hiring one's own graduates, for example, might mean creating cliques, favoring one professor's students over another, failing to introduce "new blood," and the like. And the evidence would seem to support some of the fears, for some of the great graduate departments which for years have been inbreeding have indeed become fixed in their attitudes and approaches; they are narrow in their focus rather than broad and catholic. They have succeeded in reproducing their worst faults.

But surely the taboo against inbreeding can be as irrelevant when applied without flexibility as any of the more unpleasant and specifically social exclusions, taboos against Jews or Negroes. Indeed, with the shift in the social climate on these latter matters, especially on campuses, we can find evidence of an opposite irrelevant consideration operating: many departments look specifically for Jews and Negroes, and all other things being equal, the Jew or Negro is perhaps even likely to be favored over the white Protestant. I know of one mathematics professor who insisted his department hire a Negro, regardless of qualification, on the ground that he probably wouldn't be worse than any of the present staff, and that even an unqualified person ought to be hired to make a social point. In some disciplines, I have heard the bitter complaint that only Jews can get jobs, evoking the startling echo of Jews once making similar comments about white Gentiles!

Even when taboos and other irrational standards do not operate, there is much room for subjective and highly personal evaluation. The cut of a man's suit is as important to some departments as the quality of his doctoral work. Not only do some schools carry more weight with some chairmen, deservedly so of course, but classes only a year or two apart will make a difference, like vintages. I remember hearing that Columbia Ph.D.'s before 1950 were to be preferred to those immediately after. Whether a man is married or unmarried, is a father or not, is an outdoors type or an indoor one, may (or may not) at some moment make a critical difference.

It is clear that we can expect no arrangement in the near future whereby a new Ph.D. can record his credentials on an IBM card and insert it into a machine which, after a whirring and clattering, will drop it into a slot showing the institution which needs just such a person. Indeed, any such precise fixing of qualifications might well handicap a candidate as he goes about selling himself, accentuating what he thinks is positive for one employer, eliminating or deemphasizing the negative for another. While the process of surveying the market is pretty well the same anywhere in the country, it has infinite possibilities for variation, depending on the ingenuity of the individual.

All candidates when they are ready to begin their formal career go through their graduate placement offices. (Earlier and temporary jobs as assistants or instructors often are assigned on the basis of the original application for graduate work.) Here they fill out a master form giving vital details of life and career; they ask professors to write letters in their behalf addressed to the placement office, which are supposed to be candid and confidential; they arrange for transcripts of work done at other places to be forwarded to the office. The placement office makes several copies of the completed dossier, these to be sent out as required.

While these offices are themselves theoretically supposed to be clearing houses for job requests that come to a university, they rarely get any but odd requests. Information about openings for serious jobs goes directly to the department chairman. (In the several years that my dossier was on file at the Columbia University placement office, I recall getting an inquiry for only one job through the placement office, for something called a professor of "persuasion," I think it was, at a newly formed business "college.")

The best way to be put in touch with a job, obviously, is through the professor with whom one has done his major work. Professors at graduate schools of any repute are constantly in touch with colleagues throughout the country. If they don't get inquiries about likely new Ph.D.'s in their specialties, they can simply write to several colleagues to announce that some promising students are about to graduate. This process of professorial placement works well in highly specialized areas, solid-state physics, for example, or Old English philology. But there are shortcomings to this system.

At the very large graduate schools, professors are often not likely to get to know their students with any genuine confidence. Feeling the pressure to fulfill, if only perfunctorily, this important function of their jobs, however, these professors will write excessive letters of recommendation for persons they scarcely know. "If Princeton pushes a man," one chairman reported to the authors of *The Academic Marketplace*, "I know it means I'll have to look somewhere else. I don't trust Columbia either, or Chicago. With one or two exceptions in each department, those bastards are shysters; they'll say anything about anyone to get a man placed." Of course, the obvious way through this problem is for hiring chairmen to consult directly with colleagues they know at the recommending institution to find out just how excessively the stock has been watered.

Even the academic world, for all of its unworldliness, has its handful who quickly assess the situation in terms of advancement possibilities and proceed accordingly. In a large graduate school, they learn which are the more prominent and susceptible professors and attach themselves at once, using all of the traditional wiles and devices of the sycophant. (They may, of course, be perfectly capable students, but this is beside the point: they recognize that talent alone will not get them as far as contacts reinforcing talent. Many, of course, believe that contacts alone may suffice.) If such a process does not work, then other possibilities suggest themselves: a kind of bustling political activity in all of the appropriate campus societies, gestures toward "publication" however negligible (few things are so impressive as getting one's name in print in the professional journals, even if the name is appended to a note or a book review or even a letter). But toadying and apple-polishing are common anywhere and academic one-up-manship is perhaps less reprehensible than elsewhere, for almost always it has to include some content. Few decent graduate schools long tolerate the man on the make who does not produce observable results.

Actually, of course, the big graduate schools can do almost as little as smaller ones when there are few jobs to be had. I have spoken with many Columbia and Harvard graduates, for example, who graduated in the 'forties and 'fifties, who reported that their departments had helped them not at all, except in the conventional way of writing letters to the

106

placement office, in getting their appointments. And when jobs do become more plentiful, the larger schools, many students suspect, follow a policy of empire building, of placing students where it is thought the best interests of the home department will be served. A young man I know who was graduated from one of the large Eastern graduate schools told me that he got two offers, one from a leading private university in the Mid-west and one from a state university. He was urged by his professors to accept the offer from the state university. "The only reason I could figure out for their pressing me to do this," he told me, "was that they already had some of their own people at the other place, but they didn't have anyone at the state university yet." He took the job at the private school. A graduate of Harvard once told me that his professor told him that he would get him a job at such and such a place, "because it will be good for you to be there," and did so without consulting the student about his preferences.

Most students look around for jobs on their own, asking their professors (after the basic letters in the dossier) only to push a particularly desirable opportunity. The most common way to find out what's available and where is to mail out letters of inquiry to chairmen of departments, accompanied by brief resumés, to a number of schools, selected either according to their academic standing or their geographic desirability, or both, or, for that matter, for any reason at all. (One man I know wrote to Hawaii simply because he wanted to live there.) Some students blanket the country in a form of mail-order strategy, sending out hundreds of such letters. These, of course, are simply intended to start the necessary negotiations, to elicit an expression of interest strong enough to warrant sending out the dossier.

Few jobs that carry the prospect of permanence are assigned without an interview. Ideally, schools with sufficient

107

budget ask the candidate to visit the campus, usually flying him out, usually wining and dining him in a round of parties and luncheon, dinner, and coffee-break interviews. The idea is to allow both candidate and department to get to know each other, as the phrase goes, but in fact both are likely already to know a great deal about one another. The new Ph.D. will obviously have briefed himself on the character and quality of the department before he made his application, or, at least, before he accepted the invitation to visit it. A department chairman or appointment committee that has done the proper homework knows an immense amount about an applicant, from the dossier, from supplementary telephone calls to the candidate's campus, from the candidate's undergraduate record, even from his photograph. The interview, then, is designed to uncover or display the kind of details that emerge only when one is on the scene.

The department, especially if it is located in a small town unlikely to offer the usual cultural opportunities applicants are expected to appreciate, will try to exhibit the benefits of living and teaching in the particular location. It may want to emphasize opportunities for carrying on research either through the library facilities or at neighboring government or commercial installations; the latter is especially important in hiring scientists and mathematicians.

But the department is not only selling, it is also buying. It will want to see in the flesh the candidate described on paper and over the phone. The candidate will not only be engaged in casual, informal conversation at lunch or over martinis, but may also be expected to deliver a formal lecture to his prospective colleagues.

This period of reciprocal examination is important. Not only do departments often not live up to their reputations, but persons simply turn out very differently from their descriptions in their dossiers. But frequently the point of the interview has nothing to do with benefits or qualifications; it is sometimes irrelevant to the point of farce. "He played the recorder. That was the reason we hired him." This is from a report to the authors of *The Academic Marketplace*. I have heard of instances of men being hired because they played chess or could complete a string quartet or be a good fourth at bridge or because they seemed eligible bachelors. One man flew out to a small town in the Northwest. "Look," he said to one of the men interviewing him when they were alone, "I couldn't ask this over the phone, but is there a place we can get kosher meat here?"

Most interviewing, however, takes place, assembly-line fashion, at the national conventions of the candidate's discipline. These conventions take place during the Christmas recess and ostensibly resemble the scientific and medical conclaves in offering scholars in the humanities and social sciences an opportunity to present to their colleagues the fruits of their research. Some of the conventions, especially in the physical and natural sciences, still do perform this function. But the gatherings in modern languages, history, economics, sociology (with some recent exceptions), have largely become occasions for job-hunting, hiring, surveying the opportunities, mending academic fences, almost everything except the stated purpose of the meetings.

Certainly many persons attending these meetings are actually there to discover in convenient fashion what has been going on in the various areas of their discipline. They do actually wander from meeting room to meeting room to listen to papers and to discussions, sometimes just to see a particular personage in action. They do exchange reports with colleagues at geographically distant places of work and reading that is mutually relevant. They do meet their old professors to report on their current work, and the like. The re-stimulation, the re-charging, of the sense of their whole field is not to be minimized. But even such persons are asking and being asked about openings, about salary levels, about personnel changes in important departments. And some persons, mostly hiring chairmen or applying candidates, do nothing else but this. I have known candidates and chairmen who have listened to no papers at all for the usual three days of the meeting, who have simply settled down to an endless succession of interviews.

For the candidate, these interviews are likely to be as nasty a period of his career as he may ever pass through. My experience, I have learned, was typical. I was once "interviewed" by a chairman of one of the Big Ten schools and three of his colleagues. They were gathered in his bedroom at a Hilton hotel (I forget whether it was in New York or Chicago), and they called in ten applicants at the same time and asked us to make ourselves comfortable, which meant draping ourselves on the edge of the bed, on the one armchair, or leaning against the bathroom door or the dresser. The chairman himself was stretched out on the bed, his legs nonchalantly crossed. Each of the interviewers had a batch of cards with some of our names. The "interviewing" started at once as we were asked how close we were to our degrees, what our dissertation subject would be, which professors we were working for, the cards being shuffled steadily. At one point, above the din, I heard the announcement that there was only one opening to be filled, for one year, for a junior instructor, to teach only freshman courses, and (for that time) at a stunningly low salary. I stumbled my way out of the crowded room, and I am sure I was never missed. A friend of mine was interviewed by the same group at a dutch lunch the next day. So that each professor could be exposed to each candidate, the candidates changed chairs every five minutes, carrying their plates and utensils with them.

Even this is perhaps better than the mass interviewing that takes place in one large room set aside for the purpose. Employer and employee huddle together in a conspiratorial cluster so that details of salary, course assignment, prospects for career are not bruited about too loudly. Candidates approach shyly and uncertainly to make contact with the chairman with whom they have an appointment. They try to hide, for they do not want to be found out, even by someone who is involved in the same process himself, and they often do not wish to be seen by another chairman with whom they have already had an interview. One candidate said to me, "When I go into that interviewing room, I feel like I'm in a whore house, and I'm not sure whether I am buying or being bought."

Of course, civilized chairmen interview candidates singly and privately in their hotel rooms, and they try not to go through the process of idly feeling the merchandise. One chairman, after a pleasant half-hour chat with one candidate, confessed confidentially that he really had no job to offer, but that he had liked the young man's letter and wanted to meet him to see what kind of person might be available if he were indeed filling an opening. The young man conceded to me that the interview was pleasant enough, but that it happened he had little time just then, at the convention 1,000 miles from his university, to indulge in amenities; he had to find a job for next fall and every interview counted. But there are the host of thoughtful, considerate chairmen, who are not playing games and are concerned with the profession, who tell a candidate honestly what his shortcomings may be, or advise him candidly that while there may be no job for him at their schools, they know of openings elsewhere and, sometimes, even offer to make the necessary contacts.

The whole atmosphere of the conventions is indeed that of the slave market, as the merchandise is pinched and probed and openly commented on. Peddlers and buyers haggle in usual market fashion—although usually politely. "If you get a better offer," a chairman is likely to say, "come back to see me and I'll see what we can do." Differences in job offers often get down to fringe details, sometimes significant, sometimes petty, if the salaries happen to be identical. "Our pension system allows you to withdraw all your money when you leave." "The library is no great shakes, but the faculty get reduced rates for football and basketball games." "We have socialized medicine, you know" (from some Canadian universities).

These markets are likely to be as hard on the slave buyer as on the slave. Many candidates have learned the simple art of writing good letters and filling out impressive applications, and some of these may indeed have no other talent. These persons must be separated from the more solid applicants. And, sometimes too, the sensitive and imaginative chairman will suspect that a man is better than his modest and understated application. The chairman must keep alert the most refined sense of judgment as he interviews a procession of candidates. And often he must reduce his choice to two or more equally attractive applicants, a situation that only a shrug-of-the-shoulder process can finally resolve, a bad one for good chairmen, for they are not likely to be shrug-of-the-shoulders sort of men.

Fortunately, decisions are usually not made, on either side, under the stress of the convention. Both parties return home to lick their wounds, to heal the bruises to their vanity and to their sanity, and to count up and evaluate the possibilities. A second and more leisurely interview can still take place on campus. As the shortage of college teachers has become more and more acute in the last dozen years, no applicant for a job is likely to be left completely without some sort of offer, although those at the bottom of the barrel get merely the leavings, one year fill-in appointments, offers from denominational or aggie schools which even the agencies have not been able to fill, "fluid bottom" jobs (usually from schools keeping budget down by having a permanent staff of beginning instructors: increments have to be made for only two years; then a new supply of beginning instructors comes in).

How does a new Ph.D. with several offers select the best one? Obviously, money would seem to be the first criterion, but actually the differences among the tangible details of a teaching appointment are becoming more and more negligible. Starting salaries for Ph.D.'s on their first regular job are likely to vary little among similar institutions; teaching loads are becoming more and more alike; retirement, insurance, hospitalization, and other fringe benefits may vary slightly, often according to the whims of a particular legislature governing the affairs of a state university. (Only the Ivy League schools still maintain a differential for first appointments: the salaries are generally somewhat lower, the difference presumably made up by "prestige." But even this differential is dwindling, as more schools, state and private, approach the Ivy League in prestige, and as Ph.D.'s learn quickly that they cannot live by prestige alone.) If, then, all the tangibles are equal, or nearly so, the intangibles necessarily provide the basis for choice.

Intangibles must by nature approach the infinite. They include such academic irrelevancies as climate (some persons must live in an arid region for reasons of personal or family health) or region (some cannot leave the area in which they are rooted, places like the Deep South or New England). These aside, then, the more important considerations are size of the institution, whether it offers only undergraduate work or also graduate, quality of faculty and students, quality of library, opportunity for decent nonacademic living, and the like. As the benefits of American cultural life become more and more efficiently distributed (by way of book and record clubs, even by way of films and television), more remote institutions no longer have to worry about being considered a cultural Siberia. It is the internal terrain of the institution that matters. Aside from the institutional resources, a candidate will also want to know about the atmosphere within a department, the nature of the relationships among the staff, the promise of the students.

But even after all these intangibles are scrupulously separated and weighed, final decision often depends on instinct. In a profession where one has to learn to rely from day to day on taste and feeling, supported, of course, by experience, knowledge, and wisdom, the first important exercise of this reliance comes fortunately at the beginning. A young Ph.D. I know decided on his first appointment because of the manner of the chairman. "The several places that offered me jobs," he said to me, "were practically indistinguishable as to salary, prestige of department, kinds of courses I would have to teach, location, opportunities for advancement, and the rest. The only difference that stuck in my mind was that one chairman had written me a full and obviously personal letter about the appointment; his courtesy was more than routine, he seemed genuinely aware of me as a person. I decided to accept his offer, and I have had no regrets." It is this sort of finally "humane" decision, one that depends on trusting one's heart and feelings after consulting one's mind, which will guide the professor year after year in judging students and colleagues and even the very substance of his discipline, which the Ph.D. must learn to make early in his career. And he must learn as well, almost as quickly, that luck, too, plays its own important role; all he can do is to minimize its effect, for good or ill.

LARGE
CLASSES,
SMALL
CLASSES,
NO CLASSES

No MATTER where the new professor begins his career, he will confront one paramount question of numbers: how many students will he be expected to teach every week? Some schools, in order to compete for qualified professors, have reduced the number of courses a man teaches per week but have raised the enrollment per course. But even where no such juggling of student registration takes place, the question is an urgent one. Are small classes always better than large ones? Are no classes at all—the tutorial system in England—best of all? Obviously there is quite a range of possibility between the one professor and the one student perched at opposite ends of a log, all by themselves, and the lecture classroom of 500 complete with public address system and spotlight on the professor.

It is tactless, sometimes it is considered heretical, to ask questions about class size in faculty lounges, for there is a firm belief among many faculty that the smaller the class, the more the student learns and the better the teaching. This is a proposition asserted often with the fanaticism of superstition. (I remember one outraged professor insisting that he would have to work under "sweat-shop" conditions when it was proposed that the maximum registration of 20 in his course be increased by three.) In some situations, it does appear obvious that arithmetic is indeed the main determinant of teaching effectiveness. An instructor of freshman English with 30 students instead of 15 must read and comment on twice as many compositions; a science professor with 30 students in a laboratory instead of 15 can spend only half as much time with each one in any period. But even such situations may be oversimplified, as I hope to show.

One thing the new professor learns, if he has not already learned it when he was a student, is that teaching is an infinitely variable art. Any one person will likely be very different when he lectures to a group of 100 or more from the way he is when he conducts a discussion among a group of 20. The brilliant lecturer may conduct a poor discussion; the master of discussion may fail wretchedly when he lectures. No matter what a professor's manner and method may be in discussion or lecture, they may be altogether different in private conference.

Other factors than numbers, of course, affect classroom character. Professors teach introductory courses differently from advanced ones; undergraduates from graduates; seminars from tutorials; departmental from interdepartmental courses. A professor may even teach the same course differently to two different groups of students, for just as different audiences will affect an actor at different performances, so will a class affect a teacher. In short, a professor's performance is always determined by the total context of the teaching situation.

Little of this is likely to be understood by the new professor, or understood, at least, in terms of his own experience. Indeed, his first schedule of classes is likely to seem dismal. Few new Ph.D.'s can expect to be hired for their first job to teach their specialty; they are likely to be thrust into introductory courses and to be given the sense that their duty is to flunk rather than to teach students. The new professor will probably have three classes meeting three times a week for 15 or 16 weeks (under the semester system), and he will soon find himself wondering how to relate the supposed content of the course to the textbook, and both of these to what goes on in the classroom.

It is easiest, of course, to fall into mechanical patterns, with large classes or small; to paraphrase the textbook, or even simply to read it aloud (on the obscure rationalization that the students probably haven't done their reading in the first place, and that if they did, the additional exposure in class reinforces the earlier reading); to require that certain specified facts and formulations be memorized; to consume time with the bookkeeping processes of taking roll, collecting papers, making assignments. Many instructors readily and happily adopt such patterns and stick to them for the rest of their careers; the classroom is an escape for them from having to think or even to work very hard. Stories are legion of the professors who read their notes year after year and give the same tests, of professors who forget their place in their notes and begin the next lecture exactly where they began the previous one. For such men, the size of the class matters not at all. I had a Latin professor, a genial and generous man, who allowed you to make up a cut by coming to his office for a private recitation. I went to his office once, and there he repeated for me, word for word, joke for joke, chuckle for chuckle, a class session I had not missed. He was confused about which day I had been absent. (I was so caught up by this performance that I even repeated the same errors I had made in class and been corrected on.)

Any college course should do more than merely repeat or reinforce textbook material. It should supplement and enrich this material, and if the textbook is less than perfect, as so many textbooks are, the professor should make up the deficiencies. Few things impress college students as much as the fact that the printed word, even in a college textbook (some would say "especially in a college textbook"), is not sacrosanct.

Of course, whatever a professor chooses to do, he will in some way, to some degree, be affected by the size of the classes. It is not often feasible to conduct "discussion" in a large class although questions might be elicited and answered. The Socratic method works least well with groups of 100 or more. It is perhaps equally inappropriate to lecture to classes of 30 or fewer, where discussion or question-and-answer techniques will work most effectively.

Any sensitive, responding instructor learns with experience what method or methods work best and when. Some classes first need a Socratic probing and poking to make them see the subject matter freshly and in its own character, not through the filter of an encyclopedia or textbook formulation, but they will then require an integrating lecture to crystalize their responses. Some will want an extended period of lecture, in which certain basic facts and attitudes are laid down, before they become able to deal with the subject matter in discussion.

For the professor, lecturing offers the opportunity to organize afresh and consciously his own response to an area, to elaborate on the more piquant aspects of it, to emphasize the fundamentals and skim the non-essentials; it provides students with a panoramic sense, a steady scanning as well as a lingering focus. Many professors use lecturing profitably and properly to explore new approaches to and new integrations of their subject matter, in the course of writing books or articles. The lectures of a man expert and intelligent in his field offer students the chance to see a mind at work on a bounded subject matter. They learn that standard text-book responses are, after all, only the result of earlier such attempts to understand and codify. (Of course, much of what has been said here about lecturing would apply with different force to different disciplines; little, I suspect, would apply to basic courses in science and mathematics, although even here, a skilled lecturer may find ways of arranging and orienting his subject matter that will be meaningfully fresh, and supplementary to any textbook.)

Discussion classes provide the greatest variety and the deepest of pitfalls in college teaching. In a lecture class, a student can take the measure of the professor and, if he wishes, respond with any needed grains of salt. He need not take the professor on. Even in private conference, a student can learn to evade clashing with his professor in any way. But in a discussion class, where the whole method of teaching depends on getting students to speak their minds, it is difficult to escape, to make oneself invisible. The instructor plays devil's advocate, asks obvious questions, pushes an issue to its breaking point, finds contradictions, insists, in short, on a response. Any instructor, clearly, who is less than balanced and fair, sensitive and experienced, can not only hurt individual students needlessly, he can confound the whole learning process. He can indeed assure negative responses; the reaction to a professorial bully is often a resistance to the whole subject matter. (It took me years to overcome an antipathy to mathematics developed by a sadistic high school teacher; when I did, and thought of specializing in math, it was too late.)

Discussion classes can get out of hand, with students engaged in a Donnybrook. There's a story of a philosophy class at CCNY in which the instructor kept insisting that all terms in the discussion be defined, and one hysterical student started shouting, "Define 'the,' define 'the.'" Instructors have to guard against using discussion to press their own point of view, or holding a student's dissenting opinion against him. Students commonly use discussion sessions to get off the subject, to steer the class away from the assignment, either because they have not done it, or because other things interest them more. Discussions can easily degenerate into dormitory-level bull sessions. But it is also in discussions that some of the most significant learning can be done, as students try out ideas, modulate them, switch positions, use facts to support their arguments, discover their ignorance.

Discussion sessions work especially well with interdepartmental or honors courses, where students from different disciplines are gathered. Here, ideally, one student can supplement another and can instruct even the professor himself. The interdependence of disciplines emerges through such discussion perhaps more dramatically than in any lecture.

The individual conference may be either a supplementary arrangement in any course, in which students make appointments to see their classroom professor, or may be a substitute for an actual course, that is, it may be the course itself. Here the student carries on, hopefully, a dialogue with the professor, in which there is not the same formal combat as in a discussion class or the superior-to-inferior instruction of a lecture. Compatibility is obviously important, and both students and professors may be tempted to relax under the informal relationship. Professors may be casual about making assignments for work; students casual about carrying them out. Clearly, too, the individual conference works best with mature students, those who can discipline themselves to spread out their work and not exploit the freedom from regular class periods as an opportunity for coffee-klatsching.

The issue, then, of size of class cannot be resolved simply, by any ready formulation. The teaching and learning processes are much too complex and subtle to lend themselves to IBM reduction. Not even the simple arithmetical problems have simple arithmetical answers. Will 30 students in one freshman English class do more poorly than 15 each in two classes? No answer is possible unless we know what is being done in each class and who is doing it. Thirty students in the class of an experienced teacher will probably do better than 30 in the classes of two inexperienced teachers, no matter how specific the syllabus or how standardized the tests. An experienced science professor can teach a laboratory student perhaps twice as much in half the time a beginning instructor might be able to give the student.

Professor W. Albert Noyes, Jr., who teaches chemistry at the University of Rochester, testified before a Congressional committee: "For the able student it is better to sit in a large class with a fine lecturer who is also a great scientist than it is to become intimately acquainted with instructors not worth knowing."

Nor can one long sustain an argument, I think, that more flexibility is needed in arranging traditional classroom meetings. In a brilliant essay in *Harper's*, Nathan Glazer contends "that a very large part of what students and teachers do in the best colleges and universities is sheer waste." One reason he offers to account for this waste is the classroom system. But as I have tried to show, the classroom system cannot be described as a single, unchanging, unchangeable, rigidly fixed process. The only details perhaps which are rigid (and even these are subject to considerable modification in the hands of imaginative teachers and administrators) are the several meetings per week, and the number of weeks per semester.

Within these limits, however, endless variety is possible. A class meeting three times a week may have a lecture one day, a full discussion another, a seminar-type presentation by students and professor on the third. In addition, individual private conferences may be arranged. Indeed, Mr. Glazer implicity recognizes this possibility when he asks "college teachers to honestly consider in how many courses a dozen good lectures would not do all that could be done—in the form of *lecturing*—for a class." I can answer readily and confidently: few. But I would guess that few professors actually attempt more than a dozen genuine lectures. He is absolutely right, of course, when he writes that "if lecturing is to be worthwhile it should be personal, fresh, original." Only the professors who are actually hiding from teaching will lecture all the time, and everyone knows that they only give non-lectures, so to speak, long monologues that are empty, stale, and repetitive.

The rhythm and discipline of a fixed number of meetings per week offers a valuable framework for much college work. It allows for pacing, for absorbing a subject step by step, with periods of reflection between. Few courses can be taught as well with one three-hour meeting a week as with two or three meetings of shorter duration. It is valuable for the mind to clear itself between each exposure. One has only to read the novels and biographies of students who have worked under tutorial systems, in this country or abroad, doing little of their relevant reading until shortly before examination time, to see at least one possible shortcoming of a system without regular weekly meetings. They will cram into a week the reading and studying that should have been done over a half year, often endangering their health, and perhaps not really assimilating the subject matter. (I think of *George* by Emlyn Williams, *Lucky Jim* by Kingsley Amis.) But, of course, such a system can have value, and when instituted alongside our more conventional system, can provide the benefits of individual reading and

123

study without neglecting those that come from conventional class work.

Many college departments, especially those with huge staffs, make it a practice to observe a beginning teacher in the classroom. Of course, such observation may have some practical value. One can tell whether or not a professor's voice is reaching students in the last row, and whether his speech is free of gross defects which would make him incomprehensible. Also observation can pick out the extreme eccentric. A director of freshman English told me he found one new instructor addressing a class while sitting on the floor, squatting, back against the wall. But obviously, observation, aside from creating an artificial situation, hardly takes into account the capacity for variability in any one man. To be meaningful, observation would have to be first of all invisible; second, it would have to take place over a period of time and in different situations—lecture, discussion, conference; and third, it would have to evaluate in some way how the instructor actually communicated with his students, and not just with the observer.

A new professor will have to learn to live with the particular habits of his department, but he would probably do well accommodating to every demand for his first few years, until he finds a pattern suitable to himself. Some men are born to be lecturers, some, to be discussion leaders; and some, teachers on single logs. It is impossible to determine beforehand, at least on the college level, which way is most congenial for one. It is a mistake, I think, to go to any one system in college teaching to the exclusion or slighting of any other. The enlightened institution will recognize the value and importance of flexibility, and will allow faculty to work in the manner best suited to their talents. There is no point in abolishing the regular arrangement of three periods per week for a semester, and simply going to a

124

tutorial system for everyone, or for limiting all classes to a maximum of 20, or for instituting any one arrangement of class size and number of class meetings.

If there is anything wrong with what goes on in the college classroom today, it is only that not enough different things go on, not that only one thing does. But all over the country, in private and in public institutions, the range of teaching techniques is widening enormously. Stanford University, for example, is only among the most recent schools to install a painter in residence, his studio open at certain times to students. He will have no classes. Many schools have had artists and critics in residence for many years. The University of New Mexico has for a good while now been running an honors program. In the freshman year, colloquia are limited to 15 students, and conducted by two professors from different disciplines. There is no "subject matter" as such, just a reading list of a dozen or so assorted titles. At the same school, some freshman English classes are being taught in groups of 100 by an experienced professor with the aid of apprentice assistants. The professor benefits through a reduced teaching load since he reaches more students in lecture than he would in the ordinary class of 20 or so; the assistants hopefully benefit by being introduced to some of the problems of teaching freshman English through this apprenticeship; and, finally, the students theoretically benefit by having an experienced instructor rather than a beginning one. Instances may be multiplied, and will readily suggest themselves to anyone who has been on an alert campus.

The answer for any one individual may vary, but for the academic community at large it can only be large classes *and* small classes *and* no classes.

CREATIVITY
ON THE
CAMPUS

FEW college teachers look on their work as just another job. Most choose their discipline because of some emotional or intellectual commitment to it, because they want to spend their lives exploring the subject matter, because they want to recruit disciples, because they want to participate in the best intellectual activity of their calling. Whether they dedicate themselves to the humanities, the social sciences, the sciences, engineering, education, law, medicine, business, fine arts, they are not likely to think of themselves as mere middle-men between a static subject matter and an unresponsive student body. They want to make discoveries in their field; they want to stimulate their students to see the field in all of the excitement, variety, depth, importance, which first attracted them. Indeed, many professors might just as well have gone directly into a full-time engagement with their discipline; instead of teaching engineering, physics, law, painting, writing, accountancy, the professors might just as well have chosen to be engineers, physicists, lawyers, writers, painters, accountants.

This overstates the situation, for obviously many professors could not make their way in their professional fields, sometimes for lack of drive, sometimes for lack of talent. Those who couldn't are also not likely to be good teachers either, however, and probably should not be on a campus in the first place. But for those who are good teachers, skilled in the classroom as well as in their disciplines, the campus creates a unique problem: they are simultaneously encouraged to be creative—to do research, to publish, to paint, to perform—and discouraged from being so—by heavy teaching loads, committee meetings, disparagement of finished work. The most serious handicap, however, is the notion, widespread in the humanities, that genuine creative work does not belong on the campus, that teachers should not be rewarded for it and that students should not be given credit for it, in short, that creativity is an activity of the off-campus world. (Of course, no such negative attitude applies among the sciences and in mathematics, for there "creative" work is of the essence of research; it does seem to operate in some of the social sciences, however, particularly in sociology, where imaginative perceptions and organizations are often dismissed as "literature," *real* creativity being assumed to come through the use of calculating machines.)

Let me concentrate on the problem of writing, the field I perhaps know best. The mass teaching of creative writing is one of the minor commercial phenomena of our time. Every summer dozens and dozens of writers' conferences sprout throughout the country, lasting anywhere from a day or two to a month or two. All sorts of persons with a bibliography or an editorial title to their names abandon their desks and classrooms and shuttle from one mountain retreat to another to perform as teachers, consultants, editors. Men and women by the thousands plan their summer vacations to attend "clinics" where they study, chiefly, how to get into print. The rest of the year, a multitude of correspondence schools and "literary agencies" guarantee in the trade journals to teach writing virtually by return mail.

The teaching of creative writing in a thousand independent little vacuums is in its own shabby way simply a business and has only remotely to do with the work of university departments of English. Yet it does seem to affect academic practice. Many colleges and universities seal themselves off from this plague outside their walls and have nothing whatever to do with creative writing. At one great institution in the East, a professor who has written impressive fiction, as well as some of the finest criticism of our time, has been reported as vowing that "in Hell I'll teach creative writing." His department offers no courses in creative writing, although one or two professors will arrange to consult with superior students interested in writing poetry or fiction; all students write criticism in class.

Certainly writing can no more be "taught" than can painting or any art. But as a young painter can learn the relationships of color and form by painting and looking, as a young musician can learn the possibilities of harmony and counterpoint by composing and playing and listening, so a young writer can learn his craft by reading and writing. A creative writing student must first of all be a student of literature.

Professor Wallace Stegner, a writer who teaches creative writing at Stanford, made a similar point in his astute article, "New Climates for the Writer," some years ago in *The New York Times Book Review:*

> It is absurd to wonder whether writers are born or made. They are both born and made. Sometimes born writers are made wrong by the wrong teachers or the wrong influences; there are plenty of melancholy examples in our time. Like football players, pianists, Renaissance scholars, or typists, writers are the product of original talent plus training. It might as well be good training, responsible and disinterested and in the shadow of good books.

128

But some years ago, the late Isaac Rosenfeld, himself a young writer of immense promise and substantial achievement, wrote an uncomfortably honest article in *The American Mercury* called "Confessions of a Writing Teacher." He suggested that teaching writing is a hoax. His descriptions of typical creative writing students were distressingly accurate; he knew all the cranks, misfits, psychopaths, illiterates, messiahs. But the significant thing for me in his article was that he seemed not to be writing about students who were at the same time enrolled in the more usual English courses (not that such students cannot be equally shallow in their capacities and ambitions). Rosenfeld's students were the ones who flock to the writing conferences, or plunk their money orders down in the post office for quickie lessons promising a real live literary career. These are the persons who want to write without reading. You can make a bleak little anthology of similar statements by disenchanted teachers of English and writing and find that the villains are almost always students who cannot or will not read, sometimes at all, sometimes with the necessary intelligence and responsiveness.

I don't want to try a description or analysis here of the deep-seated and widespread compulsion in the United States to "create," or just to appear to do so, to paint by numbers, to play piano if only with a music roll, to write by "proven" formula. This do-it-yourselfism is positively maniacal, however noble, and not subject, I would guess, to easy diagnosis. I have had students who were hoping to write fiction as a substitute for psychoanalysis: it's cheaper and shorter to produce a novel, confided one young lady with some insight, honesty, and an enormous problem. I think the mirage of easy money lures few, at least of those with some pretense to sophistication; many students actually like to think of themselves as altruistically starving for the benefit of humanity.

A serious impulse to write is connected with actuality. It comes with and from sensitive reading, from an acquaintance with what writers have said in the past or are saying now, with how they said it, and why. The serious impulse to write may also come from some driving need to speak out, but at least it's ready to take form with a vocabulary, in an idiom, with an intent—all of these having roots in literacy. Too many enthusiastic but illiterate would-be writers are like would-be painters who are blind from birth.

This is all obvious, of course, but the misunderstanding of what it means to be a writer is not confined to eager, bright-eyed students; it crops up in the statements of some eager, bright-eyed, and fairly estimable instructors. A veteran teacher of creative writing once argued in a teachers' journal that creative writing is a "democratic art." He specified creative writing, not just any old kind of writing. At one point he asserted that "the creative process . . . can be learned more easily than grammar and punctuation." His principal device, he said, was to assign exercises in reporting the impressions of the five senses. Another teacher of creative writing spoke of convincing students "of the beauty of Keats's phrasing, or of the power of Joseph Conrad's descriptions."

But creative writing surely consists of more than the description of physical sensations. Nor does the beauty of Keats's phrasing (whatever may be meant by *that* phrase) or the power of Conrad's descriptions—subordinate aspects of Keats's and Conrad's total shaping and conception— really have much to do with creation, which is always a total achievement, not a fragmentary one. The student of creative writing who uses only his sight, hearing, smell, taste, and touch, who works meticulously but predominantly on his

130

phrasing or on his descriptions, who sprinkles in "symbolic" conundrums (as another teacher I once knew advocated— a devotee of Joyce), but who neglects or is unaware of the final esthetic effect and need of art, the blending together of all details under the shaping influence of meaning and moral intention, such a student will never write creatively; he will turn out purple patches, snippets for Bartlett or for the Department of Picturesque Speech in the *Reader's Digest,* or, at best, good journalistic ware.

Certainly the only fit and proper place for a student of creative writing to learn what he must learn is in a university department of literature. Without discussing any of our academically unattached writers—although Faulkner, Hemingway, Lawrence, and certainly Eliot have all been students of literature in their ways—a rather cogent argument can be offered, I think, in behalf of the intimate relationship between the study and the teaching of literature and creative writing, merely by citing some well known teachers and writers: Walter van Tilburg Clark, Richard Scowcroft, Wallace Stegner, Mark Schorer, Lionel Trilling, Yvor Winters, George Stewart, Cleanth Brooks, Mark Van Doren, Robert Penn Warren, Vladimir Nabokov, John Cheever, Leslie Fiedler, Mark Harris, Bernard Malamud, John Crowe Ransome, Delmore Schwartz, Saul Bellow, David Boroff.

Life is to be found and may be observed on the campus, and from it, as well as on the road. The skills taught in the classroom and the amenities practiced, or at least striven for, in the shade of ivy-covered walls are at least as conducive and helpful to art as those of the highway and the gutter. Too many students are still obsessed by the simple romantic notion which holds that life is only lived, art is only nurtured, *outside* such respectable, bourgeois strongholds as colleges and universities. To be sure, there are many restrictive, constrictive, destructive forces at work in

131

the academy, and the hopeful artist must learn to resist these, or at least to accommodate to them, no less firmly than he deals with enemy forces in the world at large.

"The healing of the breach between writers and scholars —who are, after all, one general breed," Mr. Stegner wrote in that article, "is long overdue. . . ."

> Journalists and writers who have permitted their standards to sag or lapse and who sneeze at the dust of scholars, could use some of the scholars' care, some of their restraint, a good deal of their plain learning, and a lot of their taste. By bringing new writers inside the abbey, and encouraging the living and contemporary literature along with the great and the dead, the colleges can help heal that breach and enrich themselves in the process with some of the raw and often slovenly vitality that lives outside.

Mr. Stegner's statement seems to me so right as to make objection to the teaching of creative writing in a conventional and respectable department of English, or under its aegis, or any comparison of it to a sentence in Hell, seem whimsical—charming perhaps, but whimsical. I suppose the question, as usual, may be in part simply one of definition: What do we mean by "teaching," what precisely, by "creative writing"? Certainly the attitude toward creative writing practiced during the summer orgies or by the private charlatans, which regards writing as a trade to be taught and learned like plumbing, is not worth discussing. Nor are the products turned out under such guidance ever "created"; they are the brummagem imitations on the five-and-ten counter. But the teaching of a form of expression stimulated by a serious engagement with literature and life, of writing that is developed out of a student's apprehension through reading and practicing with the possibilities of words to communicate his own sense and experience of the

132

world—the teaching of that sort of writing is appropriate to a campus.

I would suppose that everything said about creative writing would apply to painting, sculpture, music (performing and composing), drama, and all other arts. The main point I make is that creative work of any kind belongs in a context of history. Even the most original artist must have a point of departure for his originality; he must know with his mind and with his senses the tradition of his art, which means knowing it in something of its history and variety. Obviously he can learn about all this off the campus, but then he would only be duplicating work that might be done more efficiently, more congenially, on campus. Obviously, too, he might prefer not to be limited by the usual inhibitions of a campus.

The danger that creative art might indeed be inhibited on a campus is a real one, for campuses do function by various sorts of rituals, and these may conceivably restrict an art that needs the sort of freedom not always to be found on a campus. But artists might still find themselves most at home on a campus, especially at those universities which have come to recognize and encourage the active interrelation between the teaching and the practice of disciplines. Many colleges and universities are now bringing practicing poets, painters, musicians, sculptors, architects to campuses, sometimes to teach, sometimes just to be present, sometimes to be available at particular times for discussions with students and faculty. Stanford University has set up a painter in a studio on campus, simply to work, on the understanding that at certain times he would open the studio to interested students, a minimal interference with a nearly absolute freedom. This is only one of a number of instances; poets, musicians, and novelists in residence are now common on campuses throughout the country. Both university

133

officials and the artists must of course guard against the new interrelationship becoming a means in any form of circumscribing or inhibiting the art, but even this alertness can be an educational process, emphasizing as it does the necessary freeness, whimsicality, privacy, of the artistic process.

A more serious danger is that students and faculty may be encouraged to indulge in a creativity utterly removed from the control and substance of the subject matter. Creative writing, drama, painting, may find themselves under pressures to detach their teaching from the traditional curriculum of undergraduate colleges. Some departments devoted to creative work do indeed try to get their students excused from following the same courses of instruction as other students, on the theory that drama or painting, for example, are too remote from the laboratory sciences, or the social sciences. But the whole point, it seems to me, of having creative programs on campuses is to integrate them into the total curriculum, even offering scientists, social scientists, and scholars in the humanities an opportunity to pursue creative endeavors.

Is it implausible to suggest that there is a relationship between some of the content and philosophy of contemporary physics (the indeterminacy principle, for example) and some of the efforts of contemporary painting (the flux and overflow of color, line, and mass)? Or between the subject matter of some areas of biology (evolution, sex) and modern drama (from Strindberg to Albee)? Or between some of the contemporary interpretations of history (from Spengler to Toynbee) and modern music (from Stravinsky to Schoenberg)? Or between the efforts of the "new sociology" and anthropology (Riesman, Glazer) and writing (Oscar Lewis)? (Indeed, Oscar Lewis defies simple classification as either a sociologist, a journalist, or a creative worker.)

The processes of thinking, creating, performing should more actively be recognized as essential to understanding a discipline. At a national convention of the Modern Language Association, the president of the organization suggested that no person be finally certified to teach literature until, as part of his preparation, he had created some work of literature, a poem, short story, novel, play, so that he would have a living sense of the dynamics involved in making literature. While this perhaps was hyperbole, intended to indicate how removed some teachers of literature had become from the essence of their subject matter, it is only the obverse of the argument that the creative writing student study the literature that preceded him.

While the resident artist might well be left to his own devices, called upon only to the extent that he himself is willing to contribute to any sort of teaching situation (apprentices, seminars, lectures, courses, conference time), I think actual courses in creative work as such ought to be made integral divisions of existing departments. It is an error, I think, for example, to have a drama department which does not include the study of dramatic literature, indeed of all literature. A department of creative writing separated from a department of English is, frankly, incomprehensible to me (unless, of course, the department of English is, in personnel and course work, itself separated from the study of literature, which is more than conceivable; it is actual on more than one campus). The study of music unaccompanied by a study of the history and character of music, detached from the development of some critical sense about music, isolated from an awareness of the total culture (including the other arts), can produce only automatons, however superb these may be technically.

Nor is creativity necessarily limited to the arts. Creativity is the mark of the most significant understanding of any field. The man who breaks through the traditional limits of study and belief in physics, chemistry, biology, architecture, engineering, history, political science, who cuts across borders and finds integrating principles (bio-chemistry, bio-physics, the study of literature as a sociological expression), is creative. Let us but establish the principle firmly that creativity belongs on a campus, that creativity flourishes best and most significantly in a university, and we would be able to break down some of the barriers to new and important learning. Men without Ph.D.'s in their subject matter would be welcomed (instance: David Riesman, a pioneer in sociology, is by training a lawyer); the walls between subject matters that are naturally overlapping and interrelated would dissolve (interdisciplinary specialists have great difficulty finding appointments; Ph.D.'s in American Studies, for example, end up teaching history, or American literature, or political science, or sociology); new areas would open for legitimate and exciting new study (Nathan Glazer, Ph.D. in sociology, moved into the study of cities, a subject long examined by Lewis Mumford, once a student of literature).

If we are to expect any new reshuffling of our conventional and restricting curricula, of the lines marking the boundaries between disciplines, it can only come from recognizing the important role that creativity can play anywhere on the campus.

PUBLISHING,
PERISHING,
FLOURISHING

ONE OF THE glibbest oversimplifications in higher education is that it is harmful to the profession to follow the rule that unless one publishes one perishes. This rule is often put in the crisp and cruel form of a commandment, "publish or perish," "up or out," perhaps to emphasize its heartlessness. The matter of publishing is the cause of much dispute and confusion, and, among those subjected to the ultimatum of publish or perish, of much bitterness. The combatants either overstate their case, or misunderstand what publishing involves, or choose a kind of publishing that they wish to attack. As with any glib generalization, we have only a partial truth here, and we may even find the harm in the excessively simple way it is stated.

Just what is meant by publishing? A professor, a scholar or scientist, is expected to have such a grasp of his subject matter that he not only sees areas which have not yet been fully explored or he finds that the established areas call for new integrations. In the course of teaching and reading his subject matter, he decides that he might make what is somewhat stiffly but accurately described as "a contribution to learning" by undertaking either to explore new areas, to answer questions which have never been answered before, or to suggest new relationships of known material. Publishing may properly take the form of discovery, creation, or re-ordering (criticism, new hypotheses, new classification, and the like).

In the humanities, a professor is likely to find himself working with manuscripts, old books, letters, and other such documents that have hitherto not been examined at all, or have not been examined from a certain perspective. He may propose new interpretations, offer new orientations, conceivably even "make" new objects: a historical theory, a poem, a "new" philosophical approach. In the sciences, he will establish experimental situations, arranging the unknowns in such a way as to provide original findings, or merely to confirm old ones, or perhaps even to controvert established beliefs. He will study objects anew. In the social sciences, he may work with questionnaires, with statistical data of various sorts, with documents, and he will occasionally interview small and large groups of people. The same procedures, appropriately modified by the peculiarities of a discipline, will undoubtedly be applied in engineering, business, law, education, even fine arts. In some areas, the publication may consist entirely of original creations of various sorts; there may be no other form: in painting, a canvas; in a drama department, a play or the production of one; in music, a new composition or arrangement, or even a performance.

When the professor has completed his work he is expected to prepare it for publication in one of the professional or general journals in his discipline. The man who gives evidence through publication of having pursued appropriate investigations in his field gradually establishes for himself a bibliography. It is the appraisal of this bibliography which will affect a career. This list of "publications" determines whether a man will be kept on a faculty, be promoted, be

138

given salary increments, be allowed to teach certain courses, or otherwise be rewarded in terms of the various possibilities obtaining at that time. The generalization, of course, is that the man who publishes more will be rewarded more, and that the man who publishes little or not at all, will not only not be rewarded but of course will be punished. He will "perish."

Two main objections are made by the critics of the publish-or-perish system. One is that publishing often requires the professor to neglect his teaching. The argument is that no man can pursue the necessary research in a library, devote his time to organizing it, then writing it up, and still do the job that he is supposed to do in the classroom. Something has to give, and at institutions where publication is the main criterion for advancement, it is necessarily the teaching. The other objection to the system is that it encourages shoddy, trivial, pointless, casual publication.

No doubt one can find a great deal of evidence to support both objections. Students at some of the major institutions which emphasize publishing often do complain that their instructors are far more concerned with their research than with students. And certainly many professors neglect teaching for the sake of publishing. Their careers will depend on publishing and on little else. "It is neither an overgeneralization nor an oversimplification," write Caplow and McGee in *The Academic Marketplace*, "to state that in the faculties of major universities in the United States today, the evaluation of performance is based almost exclusively on publication of scholarly books or articles in professional journals as evidence of research activity." Indeed, some institutions, anxious to have "productive" professors on their faculty, will hire men who may be notoriously bad teachers.

As for the second objection, evidence to support it can be found by a casual skimming of the standard scholarly jour-

139

nals, which, if they are not exclusively repositories of academic bilge, often contain at least enough to make the discipline seem very nearly disreputable. An extended exposure to the learned journals in any field is likely to leave an informed person disillusioned and cynical. I venture that no one would challenge the fact that much is published in the leading journals in various disciplines that is simply not worth publishing anywhere. So pervasive has become the compulsion to publish that it occasionally reaches nearly scandalous proportions. Some men are known to keep getting their name in print, with notes, letters to the editors, notices of books. However long or short, however solid or wispy, whether a whole book or a note of inquiry, every item rates only one entry in a bibliography. Some men have lost their grasp of reality and made claims of publication with no basis in fact. Some itemize dozens of works "in progress" that are nothing but stray notions.

In one of the social sciences, the measurement of publication is an annual affair, with the number of lines published by the faculty at leading universities totted up in the top professional journals. Young men in this particular discipline have insisted that articles signed by them have been rejected, but when submitted under the names of their professors were promptly accepted. Editors are supposed to favor work by established men at the top schools regardless of substance, thus creating a kind of vicious circle: those that publish continue to get published; those that don't, don't. (I have made no systematic survey of this issue, but I know that this situation is not true in the humanities, by and large, and I have been told, by fair observers, that it is certainly not true in other social sciences.)

There are even departments whose motto might well be "publish *and* perish." Sometimes this is the result of simple professional jealousy. A young man, a man without full security, will produce a piece of work which does have some merit. Weaker colleagues, but with seniority, say, or with some measure of power (a chairman, a senior professor), will resent having someone lesser than themselves appearing in print. In such cases, the culprit who has dared to try to advance himself along the conventional lines will often find himself out of a job, or held back from promotion, or otherwise punished. Of course, the attack will always be made in terms either of the unworthiness of the publication, or on the grounds that only a man who neglects his teaching could have published the material in the first place. Some departments even go so far as to hold that no man can perform his teaching duties in all of their ramifications—keeping up with his reading, meeting students informally, keeping alert on matters that are tangential to the field—and still publish. Publication is often considered as *prima facie* evidence of neglect of professorial duties. "He came here as a young man, and at the time the head of the department forbade research—said that it destroyed a man's capacity to teach" (*The Academic Marketplace*).

The excesses of the publish-or-perish commandment have provoked a number of observers, not least among them Jacques Barzun, who himself could never be charged with being defensive about publication, to criticize the whole system of publish-or-perish. They argue that it encourages the proliferation of trivial scholarship (it is doubtful whether they would even use such an honorific term as scholarship) as well as the support of slipshod teaching. No doubt this is true. But I contend that to the extent it is true, the faults of the system lie in those persons who observe it rather than in the system itself.

Let us consider first the objection that the professor who publishes, who pursues research in the library or in the laboratory, neglects his students, or otherwise does not do justice to his work in the classroom. Obviously, many professors will have a greater or lesser sense of duty regarding work in the classroom. Of all academic responsibilities, it is often easiest to shirk or fudge classroom chores. Professors can easily neglect conference periods, can read from old notes or from old books, can do nothing to make the daily classroom experience a vital and original one, a "creative" one. But there is no inherent reason, that is, a reason built into the situation, which requires a professor to separate his two duties, of teaching and publishing, from each other. They should be, and often are, integrally interrelated. This is not merely a rationalization, as some would argue. Some professors find it inconceivable to teach without doing research. Indeed their teaching grows out of their research, their research grows out of their teaching, the two live off each other in a genuinely re-creative way. It is only when no teaching takes place, or when the research is dry-as-dust, unrelated to a living sense of the discipline, that the two can indeed be hermetically sealed off from each other.

Consider a few examples. How can anyone teach English literature of any period without maintaining an active, searching, analytical approach to the subject matter? My own experience in teaching Milton is to the point. In reading Milton while at the same time reading Dryden, certain relationships seemed to me to be important, relationships which had not really been explored in all of their full import. The work I did at various libraries, relating Milton to Dryden, was intimately associated with my teaching of Milton in the classroom. A biologist studying the life of mammals in their natural habitat, publishing papers on various aspects of his discoveries, surely cannot block this material out of his mind when he enters the classroom to lecture on how mammals live in a particular locality under particular conditions. A professor of contemporary Euro-

142

pean history, interested in American attitudes toward the Soviet Union from its inception to the present, who makes a thorough analysis of editorials in leading newspapers and journals, can scarcely forget this material, or slight it, when he is talking about the subject in his classroom. Certainly as well, the professor of art history who is also a painter, who has worked out for himself some of the problems of contemporary painting, can scarcely fail to use his own living sense of the subject when he talks about modern painting.

I think it must be kept constantly in mind that, after all, the college teacher, unlike the high school teacher, say, is not merely the transmitter of a given body of information. Surely he is that to begin with. But in addition he is also an innovator, a man who uncovers new information or proposes new arrangements; he is not merely a kind of tape recorder spieling back, however skillfully, what happened to have been fed into it.

Now of course there are a good number of introductory courses in a university which often do require a handling of introductory material. How can a new instructor or assistant professor, whose teaching load consists largely or even exclusively of introductory courses in his discipline, whether it be in the sciences, social sciences, or humanities, be expected to publish? One answer of course is that many such beginning college teachers do find time to continue the research that they began in graduate school and to publish the results when these are obtained, whatever and wherever they happen to be teaching. They may be and often are considered traitors to the cause, but it is in their nature to publish.

But even if we grant that there is no time to do anything but get through the necessary daily routine of teaching, can we say that there is nothing that the responding, intelligent, imaginative young instructor can contribute? What he may

143

say may relate only to some problem in teaching his particular discipline. He may suggest new arrangements of presenting the material. He may, especially in fields where interpretation and response are of the essence, as in the humanities and the social sciences, suggest that there are other ways than the traditional ones for reading a work of literature, a sociological study, a philosophical treatise. The point to be made here, I think, is that publication takes various forms, certainly of varying legitimacy and relevance, of varying worth, but it is possible always to remain actively engaged with what one does in the classroom to the extent that this engagement results in new responses. (One recent article in *College English,* by a Lester Hurt, called "Publish and Perish," while making the point that publication can destroy one's effectiveness as a teacher, seemed to me to be controverting its own thesis by its very existence: it was a thoughtful examination of the relation between publishing and teaching.)

Now I am not arguing for a kind of contrived publishing. We already have too much of that, scholarship that has the looks of scholarship, criticism that appears to be criticism, even creative works that have the semblance of creative works, none of which has depth, substance, or validity. This is a kind of publishing which is empty and might just as well be called non-publishing, like non-teaching.

Certainly there are formidable obstacles to any kind of publishing or writing when one teaches a full academic load, whether of introductory courses, or of courses in one's specialty. This is, I think, widely recognized, and more and more departments are trying to solve at least this sheer physical problem by providing more stenographers, dictating machines, funds for research, and the like. But the best facilities, the most energetic encouragement, the most obvious and immediate rewards, can scarcely break through a kind of inanition which is characteristic of many college teachers.

Many professors have exhausted whatever creative or scholarly impulses they might have had in their work in graduate school. They may remain good teachers, they may perform faithfully, they may be dedicated to their profession. All of this we can grant comfortably and readily. But they clearly shirk one of the requirements of the profession, that of keeping oneself intimately engaged at every level, in every way, with every aspect of the field, from the most obvious to the most recondite.

As William Van O'Connor argues in another article in *College English,* "Publishing and Professionalism in English Departments," it simply is not necessarily true "that the nonproductive scholar is a better teacher.... That there are occasional good teachers who are unproductive should of course be admitted. It should also be said that many of these are both lazy and irresponsible."

Perhaps the requirement that used to be standard in some graduate schools of requiring every doctoral candidate, at the very start of his career, to publish his dissertation is not altogether without merit. A dissertation should ideally be a major contribution to the scholar's or scientist's field. Publication indicates that the work has survived the scrutiny of various experts in the field, the candidate's own professors, the editors of the publishing house. And even when the candidate subsidized publication, the work did become available for others to use in whatever way they could. Publication is a sign that the scholar is ready to submit himself to the judgment of colleagues. I remember one of my professors at Columbia regretting that the graduate school had dropped the requirement of publication. "Most dissertations now, good or bad," he said, "will never get published. I'd estimate that whatever the cost to the student of publication, he would get back his money many times. In terms of salary, appointment, and promotion, I'd guess that a book is worth a good $10,000." And this was in the early 'fifties.

But like all rigid requirements, of course, the insistence on publication became easily abused. All sorts of worthless and near worthless studies came out, subsidized by the candidates; these were simply looked at, not read or evaluated, when appointments or promotions had to be made. After a while, publication became a means of distinguishing, not between a person worthy of the Ph.D. and one not worthy of it, but simply between the person with means and the one without.

Now that publication of the dissertation has ceased to be a requirement at almost all graduate schools (I know of none that still follow this requirement), the situation has not been improved just by this fact alone. True, the poorer candidate is not passed over for the Ph.D. But publication of the dissertation is still a mark of great distinction, with or without subvention, and the difference between the published dissertation and the unpublished one is not necessarily the difference between quality and lack of it. The man who gets his work published may simply have been more indefatigable in pursuing the possibility; the work itself may have landed on an editor's desk at the right moment. Scholarly publishing, especially of books, is often subject to all of the vagaries and mysteries of commercial publishing. We must always remain concerned with the intrinsic worth of a piece of work, published or unpublished, but there is no denying that a dissertation in print, like any piece of writing in print, looks better than the same thing in manuscript or typescript, and not only to chairmen of departments and deans.

Professor Barzun argues cogently that the pressure to

146

publish has resulted, not in the expansion of any genuine scholarship, of contributions to art or learning, but in the growth of obscure journals publishing trivial little articles, which no one can read or cares to read, because the subject matter is unimportant and the style objectionable. One obvious answer to this objection, which has been made any number of times by persons considering the issue, is that the quality of scholarship and research in general obviously depends on the editors of these journals, on the supposed masters in a particular field, and not least on the writers themselves. Let the editors reject shoddy research, and it seems to me there is no question that the level of the content and of the style will necessarily rise. The problem obviously is with the levels of expectation and achievement in any particular discipline. Surely we ought have no journals at all if they are worthless, but we might almost say that we also ought not have the disciplines themselves covered by the journals if these cannot operate on a respectable level. Publishing in any area should not be lower than the level of the area itself.

Perhaps more generously, it might be contended that even the seemingly trivial articles, those that seem more like an exercise in ritual than a true attempt at discovery, contain some small glimmer of truth or vision. They may be the smallest and the dullest of mosaic pieces, but they do contribute to a total picture, sometimes just negatively, by obviating the need ever to do this piece of work again, sometimes by filling in background or border.

Those persons who study publications of staff members being considered for some sort of advancement should obviously evaluate the publication record in terms of quality and not of quantity. If so much publication is indeed merely a matter of adding up items without ever looking at them, then surely it is not publishing itself which is at fault, but the fools who are only interested in the number of times a man's name appears attached to any sort of print. Such administrative incompetents shirk their work, expecting arithmetic to do it for them. We should never suffer fools gladly, and we certainly should not allow fools to compel us to reject the whole concept of publishing in higher education because of their various stupidities and idiocies.

Publishing still remains one of the few objective criteria of college teaching. If we understand that publishing is evidence of a professor's continuing and meaningful relationship to a subject and to his teaching, of what is variously called "productivity" and "creativity," then we can properly use a publication record to evaluate a man's performance. Clearly this must be done with a great deal of discretion and restraint, and with a subtle exercise of all of the usual modulations which are applied in any measure of a person's worth. Mere quantity should never in itself be a significant measure. It seems to me equally clear that to consider publishing in a vacuum empty of teaching is short-sighted. (Obviously, of course, there are many research professors, who never enter a classroom and do not wish to do so, whose value to an institution or discipline depends entirely on the nature of their publication record. I do not have this sort of person or this sort of production in mind. The publishing which is a problem on campuses is that done by the man who remains in the classroom.) All sorts of very careful discriminations must be made. In some fields a short paper of two or three pages, turned out in three or four years, may well be the equivalent of a volume turned out annually in another field. A work of original scholarship must surely rate more highly than a collection of other persons' work, or than an edition of some obscure writer; books that are described as "contributions to learning" must certainly be valued more highly than textbooks, even when

148

these may well be important in establishing new perspectives in a field.

Nor should the failure to publish be offhandedly ascribed to laziness or incompetence or indifference. Many persons simply cannot organize themselves in the necessary ways to put together the results of their research, of their thinking, of their analyses. While the final burden of appearing in print still remains on their shoulders, it may well be understood that a creative professor has just not been able to get around to crystalizing his work in the appropriate form for publication, but that eventually it will be done. Everyone in academic life can probably cite instances of very late starters, of full professors suddenly breaking into print with substantial work. But it is likely that all along it was well understood that the work was ripening at its own rate, that "productivity" was not absent.

We might well want to exclude from any concept of publication the entirely "practical" work done by professors who act as consultants on enterprises which seem to be entirely commercial, but even here one would have to define publication generously and sensibly. For example, a lawyer who teaches, say, tax law, and is called in as a consultant by the government or by private persons, might well be considered, in the briefs that he prepares, to be involved in a kind of publication. The fact, of course, that a professor gets paid for his publication is irrelevant, in law or in any field.

Perhaps one other problem arises in defining publication, that of a man publishing in a field entirely outside his own, a scientist writing novels, a historian turning out poetry. I think it important to define publication in the present context as that which is relevant in some way to one's subject matter, but clearly this relevance should be widely and wisely interpreted.

It is often assumed that young men are the most vehement objectors to the rule of publish-or-perish, for certainly they are the ones most immediately and critically subject to it. Let me conclude by quoting a young instructor from Duke University (also writing in *College English*), who seems to have apprehended the meaning of publication early in his career. "Dedication to the ideals of the intellect and a willingness to sacrifice something of self for the promotion of knowledge," writes Mr. Donald H. Reiman, "have been hallmarks of the best teachers I have known, and although personal limitations interpose themselves, I am convinced that most productive scholars are better, not worse, teachers for their scholarly passion. Consider the alternative: a man of great intellect but somewhat introverted personality who concentrates on methods of teaching or superficial preparation for classes, rather than on deep knowledge of a field, is a teacher twice as self-conscious and half as effective because he is acutely aware that his mastery of the subject is inadequate. Buttressed, however, by the confidence that personal discovery brings, such men can become stimulating teachers as well as valuable contributors to the scholarly world."

FREEDOM,
TENURE,
AND
TYRANNY

A PROFESSOR's life is beset with insecurities, small and large, from the day he begins to think about the profession. His life is continually appraised, not only on the basis of what he does but, sometimes more importantly, on the basis of how he does it, on the basis of what he happens to be, and not always according to clearcut standards that can be trusted to remain more or less fixed. As a professor, he enters a whole new realm of insecurity. His first job will undoubtedly be a time when he has to prove himself without experience, preparation, or very much sophistication. After he does become settled in a particular job, he will have to submit himself to periodic reviews of his performance, these having the very practical end of salary raises, of promotion, of assignment to important academic duties, some of them having to do with committee work, some with administration. Implicit in all of these estimates is the understanding on all sides, faculty and administration, that human evaluation is subject to much error, may be applied whimsically and arbitrarily, and may interfere with the serious objectives of education. To counter the whimsicality and uncertainty, at least to some degree, the principle of academic tenure has been established.

At first look, tenure has something of the self-protective intention of the old guild system or of the contemporary closed shop. In brief, the principle of tenure holds that once a professor has gone through a probationary period, in which presumably his qualifications have been thoroughly scrutinized, he cannot be fired arbitrarily. Most rules regarding tenure state simply that a man may be dismissed only for adequate "cause," and then only after a full hearing, approximating an actual legal trial in its safeguards, before a committee made up of his peers.

Some of the advantages of the tenure system may surely be seen at once. Under it, a superior whose politics happen to differ from a professor's cannot fire the professor simply because of this difference. A disagreement on an academic subject cannot be used as grounds for casual dismissal. Personal distastes of various sorts, animosities that develop on all campuses, none of these irrelevant factors can be applied arbitrarily to cast a man out of his job. These perhaps are trivial matters, and it may be argued that no serious campus would allow reasons of such a nature to stand. The fact is, of course, even with the system of tenure, frivolous reasons have often been the basis for easy dismissal. Of course, these highly personal and subjective grounds for dismissal are more commonly exercised before a man gets tenure, before his probation is over, when theoretically a man may be refused tenure for any reason whatsoever.

The most important reason for tenure would seem to be that it permits a man to have freedom to pursue his academic aims without interference of any kind from superior administrative officials. This is the most important reason for tenure: it guarantees academic freedom. What this means is that when a man is genuinely original in his work, when he comes up with findings that may be at variance with the established opinions in that field, he will not have to fear for his job for being a dissenter, an innovator, a non-conformist, even an eccentric. Since a great deal of university work does lie on frontiers of knowledge, then obviously, unless one has a sense of absolute freedom in pursuing his subject across the frontiers, we are not ever likely to break into new territories.

The concept of academic freedom may even be considered to extend to the classroom, to the actual content and strategy of a daily course, where no pioneering is expected or necessarily even encouraged. A professor must feel free to bring up all relevant matters in a particular discipline, even when some of these may be unpopular with his immediate superiors or with boards of regents or with the local community. He must feel free to attempt innovations in his teaching. Obviously, also, he must be completely free to evaluate his students as he sees proper, within the usual terms of fairness and objectivity. Interference with any of the professor's prerogatives in the classroom could seriously interfere with the educational process. For example, if a professor feels constrained to give a student a good grade because of the student's family connections, if a professor is reluctant about opening up a new area of discussion, then he is unable to handle the material in the best way possible for him, consistent with the usual aims of that particular course. A professor cannot be made subject to football coaches, regents, tyrannical administrators, or other persons seeking in any way to control his classroom performance. Tenure guarantees that he will not be dismissed so long as he performs his professional duties and does not provide adequate cause for dismissal.

Tenure protects the entire university community and not merely the individual professor. Unless a professor feels secure while pursuing his teaching and research, then the entire university suffers. Knowledge on which there is any restriction is not knowledge. A professor who cannot do all relevant research, read freely, teach freely, cannot be a professor in the actual sense of the word.

The concept of tenure, which is universally applied in the United States, has been one of the significant factors responsible for the growth of American higher education. It is impossible to imagine that American higher education could have made any of the advances it has made if it were still as subject to the standards and whimsicalities of tyrannical boards of regents of the sort described by Upton Sinclair in *The Goose Step*. The academic world would be an even shakier and more slippery place than it already is without the principle of tenure. The wives of departmental chairmen and deans might be expected to have considerably more importance than they do even now in determining who will be hired, who will remain on the faculty, and who will be promoted. The academic world is no less subject to such influences than any other world in which the social relations of the persons involved play a large part. In some ways the academic world is probably more subject to irrelevant pressures, because the members of a faculty often live their social and cultural lives in one another's company. Without tenure, many professors suspected of liberal let alone radical tendencies would long ago have been squeezed out of the profession; even outspokenly conservative professors would not be safe on many campuses; in many parts of the country professors expressing other than the prevailing attitudes on such matters as segregation or unions or medical care for the aged might find themselves out of their jobs; in many religious institutions, even such mild dissenters as persons who drank Coca-Cola or smoked cigarettes might not make any career (assuming that they would want to). It is clear that the system of tenure protects the universities as much as it does the professors.

Obviously any system which makes the firing of a man other than arbitrary is subject to abuse. Faculties are filled with men who stopped performing as professors almost the day they received tenure. It is not difficult to put up a convincing show, during the probationary period, of being alert, productive, creative in one's field, of being a good classroom teacher, of being a scholar or a scientist. Sometimes, of course, this utter relaxation of one's energy in the profession comes later, after one has reached the final professorial level, or when one has reached a plateau above which he knows he will never advance. Many persons do literally stop functioning as professors. This cessation of professorial life, however, has rarely been considered adequate cause for dismissal. A chairman of a large undergraduate department once said to me about a professor just barely functioning as a sane person (periodically he took sick leave for shock therapy), who went through the most rudimentary motions of teaching, and went through no motions at all in research, that if he proceeded against that man, he might have to proceed against others. "How could I prove to anyone," he asked me, "that this man is particularly incompetent, that his incompetence provides adequate cause for dismissal, and justify this when I am asked about all sorts of other persons, about whom I might have feelings that are not so strong but who are also inadequate in the classroom? How am I going to use any sort of subjective measurement of a man's performance as the basis for dismissal? If we dismissed him, who would feel safe?"

It is even difficult, nearly impossible in fact, to move against men who are actually misinforming their students, who literally teach them inaccurate, outmoded, imprecise things. There are men who cannot give a straight date, a clear fact, some who have not read any works in their field since they finished their Ph.D.'s and consequently do not know what is going on today in their discipline, who remain very comfortably situated in departments.

In behalf of those guilty either of non-feasance of duty or of malfeasance, the argument is made that dismissing them, even making charges against them, would endanger the entire academic community. With our standards for judging classroom and professional performance so vague and subjective, it is often impossible to say confidently that such-and-such a man is incompetent, even that such-and-such a man is less competent than someone else. In fact, of course, such evaluations are made every day, but they are usually made positively: this man is superior to that man, he deserves a larger increment, he should be promoted, he should be assigned to such and such a committee. Rarely are invidious comparisons made publicly, although of course they are always made privately.

What happens, of course, is that administrators become extremely hesitant about granting tenure. Because so many men have turned out badly in the past as soon as their appointments became permanent, chairmen become overcautious about granting tenure to any new men. Academically, tenure is a more lasting state than matrimony. Some departments become terrified to the point of paralysis when they have to think of living forever with any new man. One large department I know, which had made a series of disastrous appointments too casually in the past, simply froze on the issue of tenure, for nearly ten years turning away good young men who promptly made careers for themselves elsewhere. Promotions, too, may be held up, for fear that a man will stop functioning as soon as the carrot on the stick is taken away.

Another abuse that flows from the tenure system, or may be considered as flowing from it, is that of academic democracy. Tenure implies that the professor has become independent of the vagaries of academic life. It implies also, in a positive sense, that the professor is assuming responsibility for the full import of his academic position. Now what this has come to mean in addition, at least at some institutions, is that he is not only responsible for his own courses but also for the curriculum in general, for the appointment of new members to the staff, for the election of department chairmen. No doubt this concept has much to recommend it. When a faculty is made up of leading, responsible men in their fields, then certainly these would seem to be the best persons to consider the problem of the curriculum of an entire university, to consider the question of the appointment of new colleagues and the promotion of present ones, even to take up the matter of who should be in charge of certain levels of administration. Some of the great faculties in this country do exercise this kind of control over many academic matters, Harvard and Berkeley, for example.

But at lesser institutions, the principle results in logrolling and ward politics of the lowest sort. When a department, for example, is given the privilege of electing its own chairman, the election may not be determined on the basis of talent as an administrator or distinction as a scholar, but simply in terms of which man will do the most for which group. At one of the city colleges in New York, for example, I distinctly remember elections in one department in which a small and rather unsavory clique could swing the choice of chairman by allying itself with one of the two large factions; it literally bargained for what it could get in the way of personal advantage. Of course, corruption of this sort is often associated with mediocrity, is indeed a mark of mediocrity, but even when there is no mediocrity and no corruption, some dubious results flow from the principle of academic democracy. A faculty, for example, which insists on exercising every one of its prerogatives may well be

157

spending time on matters best left on the desks of administrators, that is, to those professionally prepared to deal with them. There is no point in a faculty of genuine teachers and scholars concerning itself with such purely routine matters as buildings and grounds, the athletic program, even the question, let us say, of curriculum. Too much "democracy" can indeed be harmful in an academic community, which after all is essentially a hierarchal arrangement.

While academic freedom, tenure, and democracy are all designed to protect the faculty against tyrannical abuses from the administration, the community at large, the legislature, faculties with an absolute or nearly absolute degree of freedom and security can impose their own tyranny. This tyranny may be no less detrimental to the basic work of a faculty. I think of faculties that for reasons of pride, sometimes for reasons of politics, have been intransigent in opposition to a president who was appointed against their recommendation, and whose only object was to improve the whole status of the university community. Oligarchies may be no less tyrannical than individual rulers.

The abuses of tenure cut both ways. Not only can they limit an institution in what it can do to improve itself, but they may limit the individual professor himself in what he can do. Like too generous a retirement system, from which the professor cannot withdraw the institution's contributions, tenure can restrict mobility. The authors of *The Academic Marketplace* touch on this dilemma. "Today," they write, "a scholar's orientation to his institution is apt to disorient him to his discipline and to affect his professional prestige unfavorably." What this means, in effect, is that the man who is concerned with establishing his roots at an institution so deeply that he will not easily be shaken or toppled is often likely to neglect his development in the profession. It follows, of course, that the man who has con-

158

centrated on his stature in his discipline, who is well known throughout the country as one of the leading men in his field, need scarcely worry about the issue of tenure. He is indifferent to the protection it offers, at least for himself. He can move wherever he pleases whenever he pleases. It is perhaps no wonder then that professors of little or no distinction, or those with a high degree of "apprehension," to use the term applied by Lazarsfeld and Thielens in their study of *The Academic Mind,* are the persons most concerned with a strong tenure system.

Tenure systems are obviously not limited to the academic community. Government offices widely practice the system of tenure, and for the same reason. Government employees, like professors, can too easily be subject to whims of superiors. But I think the analogy can hold only to the extent that one can conceive of professors as equivalent to clerks, that is, doing a kind of work which has no audience and no meaning outside of the particular office in which it is done. Surely there is a difference between a postal clerk appointed by a Democratic administration and removed, or threatened with removal, by a Republican one, and a professor working in a university. A professor is, in a sense, an independent entrepreneur, with a reputation, with an audience, with a fund of "good will," to use an analogous business term, all of which make him capable of moving about, that is, of selling his services, should they be important enough to be bought, to others than his immediate employer.

The argument indeed has been sustained that the tenure system may work more harm than good. The good professor does not need it, the poor one should not have it. Administrations so irresponsible as to fire men of competence because they happen to be original or even eccentric in their opinions, because their political complexion differs from their own, or for any of the other myriad and academically irrelevant reasons, do not deserve to have good professors, and with the normal operation of the "market," their institutions will indeed go down in quality. In a system without tenure, the performance of a man would be under continual scrutiny, which, it is argued, is as it should be. There is no reason to suspect, the argument goes, that administrations are likely to be more willful or more careless of human needs than large corporations which do not have an absolute system of tenure. The argument continues that just as large corporations will reward old and faithful employees who have lost their effectiveness by finding some sort of sinecure for them, often promoting them to harmless jobs, so could universities follow a similar practice without becoming inhumane. At the same time this sort of flexibility would allow for the dismissal or displacement of persons whose effectiveness has declined so totally as to render them incompetent or very nearly so.

But the tenure system must always be applied with discretion. It is my opinion that it should probably be strengthened in a number of specific ways, to spell out the various protections a faculty member should have, for example, for the whole community to benefit from it most profitably. A tenure system is not designed for weak professors but for strong or at least adequate ones, otherwise it does not benefit the academic community at large. The prominent and exceedingly competent professor should never feel forced to move against his will, before he is ready.

But the present and widespread misuses of the tenure system, those which allow incompetent persons to remain in their positions year after year, damage both the learning process and the whole morale of the community. These perversions of tenure can be eliminated or alleviated, obviously enough, by making the identification of and the shifting or dismissal of incompetents an easier process. The catch here, of course, is how to define incompetence, how to measure teaching effectiveness or professional performance. But surely this is an issue which is not less subject to resolution than the other difficult issues which confront the academic world. It is not a light or easy matter to establish the professional incompetence of a physician or an attorney, or that of any other professional person, yet the medical and legal professions, in self-protection, obviously have instituted procedures which do measure professional competence, or at least gross violations of competence, and they do not hesitate, when necessary, to deprive their practitioners of the privilege to work in the profession. No such system of self-policing exists for tenured persons in the academic profession. (I exclude of course removals for such causes as moral turpitude and such extreme indiscretions that will themselves usually be punished under the law.)

Many university policies on academic freedom do allow for the possibility of proceeding against a man for incompetence of performance. The best policies include elaborate safeguards: the man has to be told well in advance of any charges that his work has not been satisfactory and in what ways he might improve it; the burden is put on the administration to prove that the man's performance has demonstrably declined since his original appointment; the proof must be made in terms of appraisal by disinterested colleagues, usually from another institution; and the like. But I know of no dismissal anywhere that has actually been inaugurated and carried through on the basis of such a policy. (Some such dismissals, of course, may have been arranged privately, particularly for mental incompetents.)

In part, as I have said, it is difficult to prove incompetence, even relative incompetence. The more significant reason, I think, may be found in the widespread sentiment in the academic world not to be unkind or ungenerous. Few

161

administrators, especially those who have gone through the ranks, have any inclination simply to be just; they much prefer to be merciful, to stretch sympathy and understanding to the farthest point; to protect everyone, which includes themselves, against the sort of harshness and hardness common in the business world. The strains of academic living, for one thing, may well dry up any man temporarily.

But it is not necessary, perhaps, to apply a meaningful standard, whatever it may be, with a rigid mercilessness for it to work its effect. The mere presence on the books of the entire community's expectation that all professors will carry their proper weight may well be enough to accomplish whatever change is necessary. Many professors relax into indifference because they do not sense that anything else is expected of them. I know of a number of professors who, once they were told they would get no further increases in salary and no further promotions unless they demonstrated some proper activity in their discipline, lost little time turning to their desks or laboratories if their productivity was inadequate, or to a more serious performance in the classroom if their teaching was. Some hopelessly unsalvageable remnant of incompetent professors will always remain, obviously, but hopefully it will be so small throughout the profession that, if not for their sake then for that of the whole community which regards itself ideally as civilized and humane, they might easily be absorbed. Perhaps I seem to be turning on myself, but it does seem best to me for the academic community's image, for itself and for the public, to be a forgiving rather than a punishing one, a widely improvising and tolerant rather than a strictly judging one. But we should link with an image of decency an image of worth; to project one and not the other is to make the philosophy of academic freedom and tenure seem like a selfishly protectionist doctrine only.

162

CAN A
TEACHING
MACHINE
TEACH A
TEACHER
TO TEACH?

PERHAPS the most striking anomaly of higher education is that professors have not in any way prepared themselves to teach. At least, it is the one that strikes outside observers first and periodically troubles professional pedagogues, whose concern has generally been limited to primary and secondary education. The insistence on the Ph.D., the whole discipline which a professor is subjected to in graduate school, as we have seen, has to do with preparing a scholar or a scientist, a specialist who can work in libraries or laboratories, but has little or no relevance to what the man will have to do in the classroom on whatever level he teaches. The first teaching experience many professors have is identical with their first jobs. They walk into a classroom for the first time to begin double careers, as professors and as teachers; the two are not necessarily identical: as a professor, the man will be expected to do research and make contributions to learning; as a teacher, he will be expected to transmit his knowledge to his students. Many men of course can do both equally well, but they learn how to teach, if they learn at all, entirely on their own, in the very course of actually teaching. If there ever was a striking instance of learning while doing, it is here. One young man, who went rapidly through the ranks to become an administrator, commented to me that his first day in the classroom was like plunging for the first time to earth in a parachute.

No one questions that it is important at this time in our history to make our college teaching as effective as possible. We are not only going to have more and more students, but we will have to teach all of them more effectively, more profitably. It is a kind of axiom in higher education that as more is taught more has to be taught. The area of literary study, for example, necessarily enlarges year by year as more and more writers, more and more scholars, produce works worthy of consideration. The field of physics has been enormously expanded in recent years. All areas enlarge themselves in the natural course of events. Teachers have to make decisions as to what to teach, how to make suitable condensations of subject matter, how to present what is finally presented in such a way that the student will get a sense of the entire discipline as well as learn the particularities of a single part or two. We can no longer casually believe or contend that every professor who knows his subject matter also knows how to communicate it effectively.

One of the readiest proposals has been to have college professors take courses in education as high school teachers do. This solution assumes that there is a method of teaching a college course which can be communicated to a prospective teacher. And it is difficult to counter this assertion entirely, much as college professors should like to. No question that many high school teachers would fail miserably as teachers without some preparation in the nature of their job, without being briefed in the types of daily situations they will find themselves facing and having to solve. That an argument can be made against the abundance of education courses is no proof against the fact that at least some of them do or could have value. Junior colleges often require instructors to have had some preparation in education courses.

Implicit in the theory of education courses as offering preparation for teaching is the notion, at its lowest and most simple-minded level, that the *method* of teaching a course is as important as knowing its subject matter, perhaps even more important. I think no one would deny that the most knowledgeable person in a field who does not know how to organize and communicate his knowledge can be no more effective a teacher than the grossest ignoramus. Of course, high school teachers have to know their subject matter as well as the proper ways of presenting it, but because of the sometimes excessive emphasis on technique, emphasis on content is often minimized. High school teachers frequently teach courses in which they have been inadequately prepared on the theory that all they supposedly need know is the barest minimum of content so long as they have mastered technique. Whatever the merits of this theory on the secondary level, it is simply inapplicable to colleges. Substance counts before anything else.

More importantly, to meet the issue more nearly head-on, teaching in college can be infinitely variable. What will work for one person may not work for another; groups of students differ radically; no two subjects lend themselves, I think, to identical presentations. Indeed there is a folklore about college teaching that emphasizes the range of techniques of great teachers. "Weren't you lecturing a little over their heads?" a colleague once asked Morris Raphael Cohen. "I generally aim below their levels." "I was aiming," replied Professor Cohen, "at where their heads should be." Cohen, who taught at CCNY for many years, once exchanged classes with a professor at an Ivy League school. "Don't your students believe anything?" the latter asked

Professor Cohen. "All they do is ask questions." "Don't your students ever doubt anything?" replied Professor Cohen. "They *never* ask questions."

Some professors mumble, some shout, some insult students, some cajole, some talk to themselves, some only ask questions, but the good ones can galvanize a class when the conditions are right. Their own mastery of a subject and their involvement in it pierces through any obstacle of their own deficiency or of their students' inattention. Given a class of students who want to learn and a professor who genuinely wants to teach (who also knows his material), almost nothing can prevent the learning process from taking place.

One method of preparing college teachers, which does not fall into the error of oversimplifying the problem, is to establish apprenticeship or internship systems, in which an instructor begins his career under the guidance of an experienced professor. Apprenticeship programs, when administered properly and imaginatively, provide as good a preparation for college teaching as any one could conceive of at the present time. The problem, however, is that many professors, of great experience and wisdom and skill, have no idea of how to transmit their capacities to interns or apprentices. They cannot make conscious or particular the details of their method of teaching. These arise from day to day, and the professor will usually not even bother to generalize. He is, properly, concerned with his subject matter, and with getting it across however he can. Usually he takes for granted entirely the processes by which he accomplishes his purpose.

College teaching is an art. Just as few artists can articulate their processes of creation, and cannot altogether be trusted when they do, so few college professors can make conscious, for themselves or others, their devices of teach-

166

ing. How does a particular subject matter, as special and complex as some subjects must be on the college level, make the leap from the professor across the boundary of space and ignorance into the mind of the students? It is very nearly impossible to generalize, except in the vaguest way, about the methods of great professors.

All one might want to say about the techniques of good teaching is that they somehow serve to arouse the students to engage with the material being taught, to absorb it into their bones, to want to learn. Obviously this is of little help to the beginning teacher. A student temperamentally unsuited to cajolery or to argument, or to any particular device used by one of his own professors, is not likely to be successful when imitating. He can only conclude from studying the records of famed professors that college teaching takes place in many and in mysterious ways.

Those who insist that college teaching, like any skill, can be taught may well be saying, in effect, that it may be reduced to measurable smaller skills, that these can be separated one from the other, and conceivably might even be "programmed" on teaching machines. I would not wish to argue that perhaps the most elementary details of college teaching might so be separated out and rationalized. We might well want to say that sticking to the subject matter, more or less, is one measure of college teaching; evaluating students fairly and intelligently is another; observing the necessary bookkeeping is a third. But obviously we can find instances of professors who have violated all of these details, and many others, and have still been effective teachers.

The plain fact of the situation seems to be, and it cannot be repeated often enough, that it is perhaps less necessary for college teachers to know how to teach than it is for college students to know how to learn. This would seem like putting the entire burden of the process of higher education

167

on the student, and perhaps this is where the burden does, finally, belong. The student is the one who must bring motivation, involvement, capacity to organize and absorb material; he is the one who must know how much time it is necessary to give to a particular subject at a particular time in his career.

Yet it would be, I think, unrealistic to absolve the professor of any responsibility in the teaching process. No matter how thoroughly we grant that college teaching as a whole is not subject to being limited by particular methods or theories, some aspects still remain subject to study, aspects important for any college professor to be aware of. Let me cite simply the matter of testing. Many college professors have highly subjective and erroneous notions about the comparative effectiveness of objective examinations and essay examinations. Now, there is little argument that a fairly judged and intelligently assigned essay will reveal much more sensitively a student's capacity than a multiple choice test, however skillfully and extensively composed. But there are all sorts of areas which are more profitably examined by multiple choice examinations than by essay examinations, e.g., an area of sheer knowledge. Facts, dates, statistics of various sorts, names, titles, all of these may properly be relegated to a multiple choice test, which does not require the maximum effort of an instructor to grade. To discard entirely the use of objective examinations in college is simply uneconomical. Professors should learn where to use such examinations with profit, where their use may be misleading, where to use essay questions, and the like. Many professors are subject to all sorts of subjective effects when grading essays, like quality of penmanship or of typing, and some students quickly learn how to deal with the professor's crotchets than with the course work. The experienced and sensible professor uses both types of measurements, as well as others, and is likely to be much fairer to students—and to present his subject more thoroughly— as a consequence.

Moreover, the most willing and able student will give up when he runs repeatedly into a wall of professorial arrogance, density, insensitivity, or intolerance. Professors—no less than psychiatrists, physicians, or social workers—work with human beings. They should, if they do not have the qualities naturally, cultivate kindness, patience, generosity, all the humane, civilized virtues. It is dangerously easy for the sadist and the egotist to find a ready outlet for his self-gratification in the classroom.

The realization by a college professor of the variety of ways in which students can learn, and can indicate their grasp of a subject, it seems to me, should be invaluable to any professor. Some students clearly learn facts better than others; they are more skilled at giving back to a professor what he has told them; they are unimaginative, insensitive, unoriginal, but they do appear on the basis of certain types of examinations as superior. Other students are quite incapable of absorbing large areas of strictly factual information. They integrate, synthesize, relate things in a large and original way. Such students frequently show up very poorly on even the simplest objective examination. How can the discrimination between only these two types not be helpful to the serious and concerned professor?

Perhaps what I am saying here is that a professor should himself first realize the varied character of his own terrain. He knows that he must lay out for himself the fixed geography for his venture in exploration, but he must also know that limiting himself to a given geography will mean that he sees or finds nothing new, that he is involved in a vast labeling enterprise only. The professor whose grasp of his field, whose intimacy with it, is so confident and encom-

169

passing that he is able to assimilate any sort of approach to it which is validly rooted in the geography is the one, surely, who needs least any sort of preparation in the technique of college teaching. This is the ideal, certainly, and it is acknowledged, implicitly if not explicitly, when new appointments are made, when promotions are considered. The professor with the largest, the most comprehensive grasp is the one who makes his way farthest in the academic community.

But we must often work with less than the ideal. Professors are mortal. Even for the good professor who betrays some sort of mortal lack in his teaching, some consciously expressed and realized awareness that teaching in college is not automatic, that it is not entirely instinctual, might certainly be of very great value. How then do we communicate any of the aspects of college teaching that do lend themselves to communication?

I offer no startlingly new suggestion when I say that everyone on a college faculty can learn from a more systematic, regularized discussion of the problems of teaching. Just as we can never say that our acquaintance with a field can stop at such and such a time, and that ever after we may be considered as finally learned in that discipline, so I think that the intricacies of college teaching can never be absorbed once and for all. If they could, we might then have them programmed on teaching machines. All we would have to do is put a professor into a little cubicle with a teaching machine and require him to spend, oh, say, a half hour, an hour, a month, every year keeping up with his trade. Obviously, to schematize the problems of college teaching is to falsify them. Teaching changes with the professor's growth, it changes from semester to semester, with the quality of students; it changes from course to course, it may even change from week to week. What we need is an admission on college campuses that free discussion of the problems of college teaching can be valuable, not only to the established professors, but to newcomers as well.

Nor may it be heretical to suggest that some division of the university deliberately set itself to studying with precision the problems of teaching and learning on the college level. I suppose that the history and attitudes of colleges of education make them least appropriate to carry on such study although they would seem to be the most logical; if their approaches to problems of elementary and secondary teaching are any guide, they are likely to be reductive and simplistic, minimizing the importance of subject matter, maximizing that of technique. Perhaps departments of psychology might be the place, or even departments of sociology, which have done so much to study the social nature of students. I think every college professor could use facts about how to construct and interpret different sorts of examinations for different situations; about how students learn what in particular subjects; about the relative effectiveness—for the same students with the same instructor— of different ways of presenting the same content; of the relative effectiveness of large and small classes (see Chapter 9 above); of the value of recordings, television, or other mechanical aids.

It strikes me as amazing that we in the profession should know so little about any of these matters, except in the most impressionistic way. One reason, clearly, is that up to now, up to the middle of this century, the burden of getting a college education did depend on the students. The professors were primarily concerned with enlarging their discipline. When they had to concern themselves with the problem of handling students, when they could no longer shirk the responsibilities imposed by increases in students, they responded with a certain hysteria. I remember attending departmental meetings at which dire prophecies were made about the destructive effect on teaching if classes enlarged by even a handful. Many teachers, able to neglect or ignore their students for years, have suddenly had to face up to the fact that they do have a function in the classroom that can not be shrugged away.

Professors continue to respond to new possibilities with a shrill and totally unacademic bias. When television reared its ugly head on campuses (with the body that of the Ford Foundation, which merely wanted to try out educational television as one method of resolving the disparity between the increase in the number of students and a concomitant decrease in available professors), some professors reached heights of invective. One of the most vehement objectors I knew was a man who for years had been playing records in his classes. Now, after several years of working with educational television, we can say with some confidence that the medium does not work so well with some subjects as with others, that it still needs improvement where it does have some value, and that it hasn't violated the professor's sanctity of expression, as some observers were sure that it would do. At least an objection to educational television today is based on some fact, not on fear and prejudice.

Teaching machines, also, simply scared many teachers. Some took their advent as equivalent to an announcement that education itself was to be wiped out. Yet the fact was clear to anyone who looked into the claims made by the teaching machine experts themselves that these devices would release many teachers from slave labor, the dreary drilling of clearly delineated areas: introductory courses in English, mathematics, sciences, history. They will never replace the teachers of courses where learning is not a neatly fixed process, where originality and imagination mark the teaching and the learning.

172

It is paradoxical that professors, who fear so much that they might be replaced by machines, when a practical expression of their sense of their profession has to be made, prefer not to think of themselves as teachers. They prefer to join organizations of scholars and scientists rather than of teachers. It is more prestigious to read a paper at a meeting of the Modern Language Association of America than at one of the National Council of Teachers of English, or to publish a paper in *PMLA,* the journal of the former, than in *College English,* that of the latter. College teachers want nothing to do with high school teachers of their subject, failing to join organizations that include both, while, of course, they go on complaining, and often legitimately, that high school teachers do not adequately prepare their students for college work. Yet, there are organizations where liaison between the high schools and colleges could be established, in which the high school representatives ask nothing better than to be told how properly to get students ready for advanced work.

Many professors consider students and classes one of the curses of their profession. We have seen that one of the highest rewards offered today to the professor of distinction is a contract that specifies no teaching, no student responsibility. And many professors, even those who enjoy and are proficient in the classroom, hunger after similar rewards, small classes, fewer classes, or no classes at all.

Teaching is really not quite respectable on a campus, partly because it takes place, with all of its burdens, on the lower levels, before the students take over and begin their own processes of learning; partly because many professors actually find it difficult or impossible to teach anything (I remember one mathematics professor who used to look at a difficult calculus equation, close his eyes, and give the answer; he never did know how he got the solution,

173

and of course he never could tell students how to get it);
partly because it is difficult objectively to evaluate effective
teaching. One immediately practical result of any systematic
study of college teaching would be to establish meaningful
standards by which to separate the best teachers from the
worst, which would allow for a just reward of good teaching, as just at least as that for significant publication.
Poorer teachers, obviously, need not be fired; they need
simply not be rewarded in terms of their teaching, just
as non-productive scholars are not rewarded, and they might
be assigned to work that they could do more effectively:
research, for example, or administration.

I am not sure that we can properly speak of "improving"
college teaching as though it were one single process although we might properly continue to speak of any individual college teacher improving his teaching in some
specific way. What is required, more accurately, is an improvement of the effectiveness of all college work, which
obviously involves other activities and areas than merely
teaching. Teaching is enmeshed with such problems as that
of size of class, research and publication (or other productivity), content of course work, the attitude of the community toward the colleges, the quality of students, etc.,
etc. But certainly teaching is not to be slighted as it has
been. The profession must recognize it as central, as the
ultimate function of higher education; however teaching
takes place, there would seem finally to be no other reason
for universities to exist. All work in the laboratories and libraries, however far removed from any particular student,
eventually must filter down to students to have value, to be
applied, to be perpetuated.

THE
SMALLER
SOCIOLOGY

EXCEPT in a large metropolitan area (New York, Boston, San Francisco, Chicago, Philadelphia), the social life of a college community is a closed one. The faculty depends on itself for company at dinner and cocktail parties; the unattached men squire the unattached (and sometimes the attached) women, undergraduate, graduate, or faculty; the families with children go on picnics or have outdoor barbecues with other families with children. In small cities and towns, the movie house which shows foreign films is a gathering place for professors and students, as are the local drug store, the local bar, the local bookstore, the local supermarket, even the doctor's and dentist's offices.

The mingling of faculty, of course, is often not a matter of inevitability, but of choice, and it is not unusual at all for professors at Columbia, say, or at Berkeley, which are located in huge metropolitan areas, to number their colleagues among their intimate and regular friends. While persons in other professions are happy not to talk shop during their periods of recreation, shop talk is often the essence of faculty gatherings; it provides an excuse for a kind of gossip which approaches true analysis in its intensity, and analysis and interpretation are the skills so many professors cultivate in their classrooms. They live by them in and out of class. Professors, like aliens in any country, want to stay together; they speak an idiom often mysterious to outsiders: professors of law often find it easier to communicate with professors of fine arts in the university than with practicing attorneys outside; professors of English with professors of mathematics than with practicing writers. Many professors, of course, may move in two worlds, that of the university and that of a community outside which may be defined in various ways: golf or tennis partners; neighbors; congregation; etc. But the university world remains for many the main if not the only one in which they are comfortable and, unless a professor removes himself from it for various reasons (often thus affirming his consciousness of its dominance), it is the one which shapes, sometimes controls, his extra-curricular life.

It is an intriguing world, so compelling for creative persons in its midst that they often find themselves writing fiction and essays about it as though they were anthropologists living among a strange people. Some become obsessed by its values, intrigues, jealousies, and think it a hell. Some cannot conceive of any other world in which they might be comfortable; there are stories of professors who, once they achieved tenure, never set foot outside the university town: it was their final, their permanent abode, hell or paradise.

If we exclude the colleges and universities in Siberia (the small, still hard-bitten denominational institutions; the separate teachers colleges; most junior colleges; the state colleges which in spirit and fact still remain aggie schools, whatever their new names), we find that the values, manners, styles, atmospheres, tones vary little from one school to another. The subjects of discussion at the University of

Vermont and at Antioch College, at the University of California, in Los Angeles or Berkeley, and at the University of New Mexico, at Dartmouth and at Colorado College, are often the same, and so are the attitudes, and perhaps the conclusions. Faculty is concerned with itself, with its work, with students, with the subject matter.

Perhaps this is both what is good and what is bad about the claustrophobic life faculty leads. One can leave one's campus and travel 2,000 miles to another campus, and if one finds his way properly into the inner circles, pick up a conversation or an argument he has left off at home. It is no wonder that so many fictional observers find the academic world stultifying. "But surely, reasoned Schneider," the hero of Stringfellow Barr's novel, *Purely Academic,* "no matter what zenith of social gaucherie a faculty might attain, might they not still want, however haltingly, to exchange a few ideas? ... The fact is, thought Schneider, my profession is uniquely organized for the destruction of conversation and the production of bores."

It is perhaps not so much a matter of the profession being organized to destroy conversation and produce bores as that it does not immediately, cruelly cut them out. Advertising, law, publishing must have their bores and mediocrities, but they are not suffered gladly, or at least not permanently. Academia, by and large, remains gentle and generous with fools, cutting them, if at all, imperceptibly and slowly. It is less necessary, as a way of life, for example, for a professor to submit himself to the blathering of his chairman or dean than for a young copy-writer to kowtow to a vice-president, or for a young director in Hollywood or on Broadway to play yes-man to a producer, or for a salesman to demean himself before a businessman. Except among the fools in academia, independence of character and of thought are respected; one can differ vigorously with equals

177

and with superiors on matters of substance so long as these differences remain within the bounds of academic propriety, which is merely to say of civilized dispute: limited to the issues, not stooping to *ad hominem* attacks, respectful of the facts.

It is easy to paint the academic world black, and easiest for those persons often most comfortable in it. Just what was Professor Schneider himself contributing to the intellectual vitality of his campus, besides thinking the particular way he did? And where did Mr. Barr himself, who sees some details of that world so sharply and shrewdly, so mercilessly, get his impressions except on a campus? His very book, accurate and perceptive enough in details, happens to constitute in its own being a contribution to the conversation, and it is anything but boring. Barr misses the forest for the trees.

Even Mary McCarthy does not bring off a portrait of a small corner of Hell in her novel, *The Groves of Academe*. Vicious, foolish, naive, affected, shallow as her professors are, the whole impulse which gives the novel its narrative energy is a generous one: retaining a dubiously competent professor who, knowing that he is about to be fired, claims falsely that he is a member of the Communist Party. Lionel Trilling, in his masterfully conceived short story, "Of This Time, Of That Place," concerns himself, among other things, with the nastiness of the undergraduate operator. But even if we grant that politicians are one of the sources of rottenness in the academic world, as I think we must if we take politician in its import of concern with appearance only, there is at least Professor Trilling himself to sight him and mark him and warn the rest of us.

Villains and villainies abound. I would guess that every academic has his own collection of horror stories; the fiction and the reminiscences about campus life are usually filled with atrocities. And there are indeed all sorts of situations which naturally give rise to abuse. The man dependent on preferment is a ready victim of callousness and injustice. A doctoral candidate I knew, waiting one Spring for his reappointment for next year, was told on Wednesday he had another annual contract, and on Friday that he was being let go. The chairman, otherwise a decent man, had been pressured to hire someone else, someone backed by a political faction on which he had to depend for re-election. A common scandal is that of a senior professor presenting a student's work as his own. It is easy for one person to use his superior advantage over another in the academic world, for all relationships are hierarchal: student to professor, professor to chairman, chairman to dean, *ad infinitum*.

Because of the omnipresent opportunity to be indecent on a campus, the decencies are all the more sensitively observed by decent persons, and my experience is that university people tend to be decent rather than rotten. The imperative of the university mystique requires it. Decency finds its own level, its own environment. My friend who was not rehired got himself another appointment, a better appointment, and his friends too, responding to what happened to him, also moved on to find better worlds. The department itself still has not risen above the level it deserved, that of a fifth-rate neighborhood ward run by small-minded politicians (although I understand that in reaction to this past of indecency, a group of young Turks have been trying to clean up the place).

It is impossible for any professor long to survive on robbing others; parasitism destroys itself. Rollo Walter Brown, in a reminiscence of the great George Lyman Kittredge, gives that professor's response to an incident of academic piracy. A student reported to Kittredge that his professor at another university had promptly taken an idea of his and given it to another student. "Don't let the matter trouble you for one minute," Kittredge advised his student. "And don't modify your plans—not by as much as a hair. Scurvy business of that kind doesn't work out—in the end. It is not the other man's idea; he is working at it because his chief suggested it to him. He will make little of it. The idea is yours, from the inside of you, and consequently you will be aware of all sorts of possibilities in it that the other man, whoever he is, will never see." After things developed as Kittredge predicted, he said: "We have to count on its being like that." Exactly; academic achievement comes from within a man, where it is created; it cannot come from a transplantation in a foreign host. I have always been skeptical of accounts of this sort of academic dishonesty, for I could never imagine that the thief could build a respectable structure without his own foundation.

As for the stories of professors taking carnal advantage of students, they would seem to be few, and in most cases the advantage was mutual. The authors of *The Academic Marketplace*, a factual account, report few instances of faculty getting into "trouble" with undergraduates, and none at all of them being involved with graduate students.

> If the small talk of the procession is to be believed, scandals resulting in terminations almost always involve sexual offenses against undergraduate students. (Graduate students presumably are able to take care of themselves.) Although there are stories on every campus about the professor (of either sex) who seduces his students (of either sex), there are few tales told of the professor who patronizes call girls or is "repeatedly" arrested for disorderly conduct.

It is the fiction that has established the myth; I can think of no academic novel in which some sort of faculty-student hanky-panky has not taken place. Most college students

180

are, after all, adults, or nearly so, even by legal definition; human beings thrown together will respond as human beings; what happens then is usually private and sensible and most of the time entirely respectable: marriages are common between faculty and students.

For all of the bleakness and meanness some of our novelists insist on attributing to the campus universe, it is not reasonable on the face of it to find campus life other than potentially congenial for professorial types. Professors do read, they do talk, they must appear to be using their minds. Of course, we do find academic zombies everywhere, but the *possibility* for everyone is to remain alive. Even when the living may not be very intense, intellectually or emotionally, it can never be worse than, say, life in an advertising agency or in a Hollywood studio, places with which professors like to compare universities.

In a sense, of course, the amiable tolerance which might be considered as the distinguishing attraction of campus life is exactly what keeps that life from ever rising above a general level of amiable mediocrity (which is at least better than vicious and vindictive mediocrity). Bernard Malamud, in his novel *A New Life*, sees this. The book, described by a colleague of mine as a history of the "picaresque schlemiel," genus academic, is set in the Department of English of a state college of agriculture in the Northwest. One would not expect such an institution to harbor a particularly exciting or creative department in any discipline, and such is the case. But Malamud's attitude is kind and broad in its understanding; we see no outright villains; we find no outrages; but we also wallow in a routine world of dullness, shabbiness, routine repetition, relieved only by the wildly or pathetically funny scrapes our schlemiel hero gets into as he tries to become a person, both privately and academically. Other novels—Carlos

Baker's *A Friend in Power,* with its account of how a president of an Ivy League school is chosen; McCarthy's *The Groves of Academe,* with its cutting account of how old-fashioned and simple-minded liberalism can destroy itself on a campus; Stringfellow Barr's mordant and contemptuous dismissal of just about every aspect of life on a second-rate campus—may tell us more about specific corners of the academic landscape, but Malamud's study offers up to now the fairest panoramic view, at least of the mediocre, run-of-the-mill landscape, which after all is the most common one.

As a genre, academic novels, for all of the implicit promise of the form, are thin, so thin that it is hard to imagine any but insiders finding many of them impressive. Some of the noted works are scarcely thought of as "academic" novels at all although they may in large part concern themselves with the subject matter usually thought of as belonging to the academic genre: *Crime and Punishment* is about a student, who, it is true, spends little time in class; *Portrait of the Artist as a Young Man* and *Of Human Bondage* are more properly "novels of development" than academic novels, however much development the heroes might do in class.

Most so-called academic novels focus narrowly on the campus and on campus types; they are as restricted in geographical and social range as a Trollope novel, but they rarely display the ironic vision that enabled Trollope to see among his clergymen and their ladies a wide spectrum of human possibility. One is aware in Trollope, if the characters are not, of the larger world of which his microcosm, self-contained though it may be, is only a part. C. P. Snow's carefully delimited study of intrigue at Cambridge, *The Masters,* lacks the dimensional depth of Trollope. Like so many other academic novels, it speaks first a private language to other academics, who, knowing so intimately the lines the problems take, knowing the types involved, breathing the same air wherever they may be, provide the necessary shading, fill in the relevant depths. If academics were not so influential in affecting opinion of those who buy, read, and talk about books, it is not likely, I venture, that as many academic novels would be published as are every year in the United States and England.

One of the popular sub-types of the genre is the murder mystery laid on a campus; its popularity suggests, I think, one of the underlying reasons for the genre's thinness. Academic novels do not get down to the hard essence of academic life. It is easy enough to write a novel of scandal, a novel with a key, about a particular locale, taking out one's bitterness in character assassination, or even in straightforward revelation about atrocities and abominations, but generally one wants to remain in academic life somewhere, and after his exposé the novelist merely flees to another refuge. Often, too, a wounded department, out of pride, pretends not to see the point. Malamud simply moved east from Oregon, but, of course, he was not even trying to cut through to the anthropological heart of the academic body. Carlos Baker's study of academic life was so polite that he did not even leave his campus. Barr's work defeats any purpose of serious art by being so unrelievedly a caricature. McCarthy did leave academic life and, presumably, had no strings to preserve, private or otherwise, and her work does not suffer, at least, from genteelism. But she wrote about the academic country after the merest tour through it, like Simone de Beauvoir, the lady writer from France who wrote about American civilization after hop, skip, and jumping through the United States. For all of their surface brouhaha and promise of revelation, academic novels have none of the depths and mysteries of James, Conrad, Forster, Faulkner, Hemingway. (One of the dreariest literary studies I have ever read was about the academic novel.) Murder provides spice to otherwise bland and familiar dishes, especially if the victim (or the murderer) is a type whom it is a pleasure to despise. Other varieties of spice are problems involving academic freedom, ambitions thwarted or fulfilled, or details of sticky sexual affairs, but the spice is rarely blended into the serving so that we don't bite into it.

I don't think I am suggesting that an academic novel to have substance should muckrake, "should expose academic life for what it really is." There's nothing terribly sensational to expose. That's the point. The life is bland, usually quite dull, with artificial, self-stimulating little alarums suddenly agitating a handful here or a handful there. Perhaps a novel to have the appropriate substance of art should indeed concentrate on this dullness, anatomize it scrupulously; perhaps that would be exposure enough. Recording intrigue does not quite do it—unless one could work with Trollope's tools.

I think by isolating the academic from the general, by making too much of it, we make too little of it. Willa Cather's *The Professor's House,* to my taste the best academic novel I know (yet still not altogether a successful work), transcends the form by being concerned with the character of a man. The university setting is almost incidental and, indeed, shares emphasis with the alien and primitive landscape of New Mexico. The academic novel, like any sociological novel I suppose, remains sociology first. As such, of course, it tells us more about a society than about humanity. It is too bad that we could not have a Faulkner ruminating about a campus. Perhaps my taste is so jaded, my appetite so intense, that I think Malamud may go beyond Cather with the academic novel if he chooses to, for he sees the person first before he sees the setting, and he sees them both, then, in interaction.

Taken in its entirety, and at its best, the academic landscape might be summed up as modest—modest in its pretensions, in its ambitions, in its tastes. The magazine which most neatly captures its range is *The New Yorker,* both in its successes and its failures. *"The New Yorker,"* the late Robert Warshow once remarked, "has always dealt with experience not by trying to understand it but by prescribing the attitude to be adopted toward it. This makes it possible to feel intelligent without thinking, and it is a way of making everything tolerable, for the assumption of a suitable attitude toward experience can give one the illusion of having dealt with it adequately." Professors adopt attitudes toward everything; the campus is a treasure house of the proper liberal opinions at any moment in politics (usually a little left of the Democratic Party), of the current popular tastes in furnishings and decoration (stark Swedish-type modern when it goes beyond advanced borax), of the fashionable at the high middle-brow, or low high-brow level in all details of living: serving dinner, running cocktail parties; installing hi-fi sets (sometimes only to listen to records of train crashes); hanging reproductions of Picasso or Van Gogh on walls; wearing sheath dresses or Brooks Brothers-cut suits. The almost universal admiration of classical music on campuses is symptomatic; it is a proper expression of interest and, of course, pleasant to listen to as background for cocktails; most importantly, music requires little intellectual, articulated response. Modern art and literature offer problems, and most campus persons, I venture, do not know what to make, even today, of Jackson Pollock or of Ionesco.

My impression, however, is that outright philistines on most campuses are few, and Babbitts even fewer. Those professors who can only live by the values of philistia find

185

their way off campus rather quickly. Not that we cannot find our dim, dull, and altogether colorlessly proper citizens, but if they do not quite respond to civilized ways, they nevertheless vaguely respect them. They do not sneer or guffaw or think themselves superior. And, in turn, they are not contemned or ostracized (deliberately or in effect).

The main influence on the American campus may well still be the force of the 'thirties, when the Depression permanently marked the character of all young persons subject to its effect, and most deeply, perhaps, marked those who were to make academic careers for themselves. It is remarkable how a study of what professors think and feel, consciously and unconsciously, some thirty years later, that conducted by Lazarsfeld and Thielens in *The Academic Mind*, should still center around the concerns of the 'thirties: security, civil liberty, liberalism (here referred to as "permissiveness") as opposed to conservatism. The young people of the 'thirties (and, by a not too great extension, of the early 'forties) came to awareness, first, in a world of economic uncertainty, in a world where the guarantees of tenure in government jobs far outshone the attractions of more daring if more self-fulfilling careers (in business or in art). Then, with some security attained, with work invested in a career, the whole world erupted into the insecurity of war, an insecurity made permanent by the atom bomb. In middle age, in their forties and fifties, our professors still suffer from "apprehension," as *The Academic Mind* calls it, recording it in various forms. "Apprehension" and the physical effects of it—a generalized, free-floating nervousness; ulcers; stomach tremors and flutters every spring, when salary increments and promotions are announced—are occupational hazards.

The academic life still attracts few adventurers. We get solid types, men and women ready to devote themselves

186

doggedly to getting their doctorates, submerging individuality as necessary, first, in graduate school, then on the job. The boldly conceiving types, the men who quickly grasp the fundamentals, who absorb what is best in the past, and then leap into the future, with new discoveries, new arrangements, new speculation, go into business, publishing, editing. I think of the bright young men at Columbia and at CCNY, a decade younger than myself, spared from Depression and war, who have chosen to found new enterprises, to edit magazines, to write, or to go to Washington. Those who have opted for the academic life are few, but their styles are characteristically different from their elders: they sneer at the conventional doctorate; or, having it, they promptly break into new territory; their energies constantly crackle with fierce ambition. There's nothing modest about this generation, but it is not yet fully in command of the scene.

Of course, there were the heroes, the intellectual barons, of the 'twenties and 'thirties also. They, too, lived through the academically bleak 'twenties, the Depression, the war, but by force of character, personality, and talent they rose above their fellows and established standards of seriousness and achievement that remain unchallenged. Perhaps there were fewer temptations to compromise high academic ideals; perhaps the thrust to drive high was stronger. It was, after all, easier to pursue "useless" knowledge when there were fewer possibilities to apply "useful" knowledge; once committed to the academic intention one stuck to one's field: there were fewer diversions to make one digress. The conditions do not seem so propitious today to nurture a Kittredge, a Nicolson, a Krutch, a Trilling, a Barzun, a Morris Raphael Cohen, a Cleanth Brooks, a David Riesman. But perhaps it is too early to tell, and, in any case, their examples remain. And the main point, I think, is that heroism

187

in the past was measured almost exactly by the enormity of the obstacles overcome; what produced heroism also produced mediocrity. Today, we have fewer forces making for mediocrity, and consequently fewer opportunities for heroism. And, in defense, we blind ourselves to heroism or deny and demean it.

Most campus citizens feel most at home with one another; perhaps, if they could tear themselves away, learn to live alone, they might have to cultivate the satisfactions of achievement, which is always a solitary state. They have more occasion to be at home with one another, of course, but they also make the occasion. The camaraderie of graduate students, for example, is the most serious obstacle to serious work they must overcome. The coffee shops and bars around any major university provide at all hours of the day a congenial place for talk, for contact, and students have been known to spend more years in palaver than in attending classes or visiting the library. Anyone who had to drag himself up from the Lion's Den at Columbia to finish a paper due in a course knows one reason why the doctorate at that institution used to take so long. Professors love to drop into one another's offices, hold drinking parties, meet students at the union. A campus person seems almost to fear being alone; he seeks solace or security, perhaps reassurance that he really is on a campus, in the company of colleagues. There is no *gemutlichkeit* like campus *gemutlichkeit*. If he is going to live on a campus, he may as well take advantage of the available pleasures, such as they are. No one drives him but himself.

The price is paid. The perspective of the larger intellectual and scientific and artistic and political world is replaced by a provincial view. Jealousies become familial in their sharpness and immediacy. Values narrow; one's sense of proportion shrinks. Sometimes the psychology of the aca-

188

demic population resembles that of Kafka's world: apprehensions intensify, self-regard depends on trivialities (why was I not invited to the chairman's cocktail party?), paranoid distortions flourish, one-up-manship is practiced (name dropping is common as are casual references to one's publications or instances of praise; some professors leave erudite and recondite jottings on the blackboard to impress the persons who use the classroom after them), students become objects of sadistic retaliation (no student has it worse than the student of a professor scorned by his colleagues), prominent professors become objects of casually nasty slander.

There are ways out, of course, not just from Kafka's claustrophobic closet but also from the larger and purer but still small campus chamber. A man can simply remove himself from the company of immediate colleagues and choose to live in the world of his discipline. A discipline can be as constricted an area as a campus, of course, but it is another world altogether, and it does not exclude the possibility of finding some social context to move in, a family, neighbors, colleagues in the discipline but on another campus or in a library or laboratory. Every professor is aware of some colleagues only as names; these men tend to their work, they raise families, but they have separated themselves from academic society.

Of course, as a school improves, it encompasses more, it opens the horizons; even as it merely grows, the sociology changes, includes more persons, different persons. Some campuses, acutely aware of the isolation that a faculty and student body can fall into, make every attempt, as part of the educational program and not merely with the object of recreation, to bring in personages from the outside world. Columbia University sponsored a series of seminars on its campus which included not only professors from nearby institutions but important lay persons from all segments of our culture.

One danger of campus life is that it can become as ritualized, as narrow, as superstitious as that of any isolated people, as that of some primitive race on a South Pacific island. For all of their reservations, professors find campus existence basically congenial, but it should at least overlap, if it cannot go so far as to place itself directly into, the larger dominions of civilized man. And always someone somewhere should strive to make true heroism not only a momentary possibility but a universally understood ideal.

ONWARD
AND/OR
OUTWARD

THE ONE never-ending struggle in academic life is for status. Here and there someone settles in at a low level, simply to do the same job till retirement: some teachers of freshman English, for example (who will often have been outstanding high school teachers), or instructors of basic courses in a science. These persons join a faculty as instructors or assistant professors and remain so permanently, receiving only the usual cost-of-living increases or salary adjustments within rank. These instances are so rare as to be beside the point. The dominant way is ever to strive upward, within the same institution or elsewhere (which is to say outward). As plants turn toward light, wherever it may be, so professors turn toward recognition.

Within an institution itself, the way upward is not much different from that in any large organization, an advertising agency, a publishing house, a government bureau. The dynamics of internal success have apparently become much the same anywhere. In hierarchal organizations, similar types of persons have similar chances for advancement. The sober, judicious, compromising, quiet man moves ahead faster than the impulsive, brash, aggressive, extreme one, if all other things are equal, all other things including quality of work and of mind. When all other things are indeed equal, the former perhaps deserves advancement over the latter, for he is easier to live with (and faculties talk as much about living with one another as husbands and wives, lovers and mistresses). Often all other things are not equal but are only made to appear so; mediocrity is more often the handmaiden of sobriety than is brilliance.

Steadiness, too, is prized alongside sobriety and judiciousness. The man who regularly attends faculty or committee meetings, even if he contributes little or nothing or less than nothing (inane comment that simply prolongs meetings and keeps working faculty from more important work) gets a reputation for "participating" in faculty affairs more readily than the man who attends infrequently, even if on the occasions he does appear he has something positive and even important to say. Almost by default of the intelligent and productive persons, who cannot bear to waste time on trivialities, the bustling and bumbling academician has taken over responsibility on many campuses for important matters. Fortunately he works little harm, for generally he can be depended on to leave things as they are, or at worst get involved with irrelevancies.

After all, professors can judge other professors best, especially outside their own discipline and especially when no publication is involved, at general faculty meetings or in smaller committees. It does not take long, if one cares to, to master the fine art of seeming to participate meaningfully in meetings without really straining one's intelligence or offending one's colleagues. After a discussion has naturally crystalized itself, one can always sum up. One can always ask questions to clarify a point, then nod intelligently whatever the answer. (The game is played usually by more than one party, and not infrequently a chairman himself will answer with double-talk a question posed in double-talk;

both questioner and answerer then seem especially intelligent to everyone else who can understand neither.) Always there are parliamentary tricks to pull; these demonstrate that one has been following the discussion and knows what point the complicated series of amendments to amendments has reached, and whether the motion itself is being voted on, or the amendment, or the amendment's amendment.

Prestige is thus often built on manners, on signs of accomplishment rather than on any accomplishments themselves. Prestige may also be built on hearsay. Name-dropping is a highly developed technique. If one can casually indicate that he has been in the company of the great, then obviously some of the greatness is thought to rub off on him. No one ever checks such indications; they are not even like bibliographical listings, which one can at least look up in a library if one cares to. One talks about how successfully one has been teaching in class; how popular he is with students, poor ones and good ones; how students clamor to enroll in his courses even though he gives more F's (or D's or C's) than any other instructor; this serves also to show how much softer the other professors are. (This technique is suitably modified if statistics on grades are distributed, and idle claims become subject to verification.) Sororities and fraternities may often be counted on to cooperate; many campuses have annual elections of "best" or "most popular" (or "handsomest" or "best dressed") professor, and while it may not be accurate to say that some professors "electioneer" for such distinctions, it is not inaccurate to say that they do not discourage them, and that usually the same types are chosen year after year (boyish, enthusiastic, sentimental, gregarious, and unproductive).

The devices of academic ascension vary enormously, and may never be definitively described, for someone ingenious will always come along and introduce a new ploy. But I

193

think it can safely be generalized that campus one-up-man-ship is practiced most energetically and successfully on those campuses where substantial measures of accomplishment are lacking. Usually, this occurs on poorer campuses, of course, whose faculty and administration do not trust themselves to evaluate a man on his intrinsic worth. These campuses almost always overvalue men outside (perhaps accurately, for they must sense their own inadequacies). At such places, only the signs count: the number of items in a bibliography, one's manners at parties and meetings, the capacity to be oracular without commitment, news stories in the local press, anecdotes about meetings with celebrities, and, perhaps most importantly, offers from other institutions. At a school which has no sure way of telling who is worthy in its own midst, the dependence on what other schools think has become nearly the determining standard. Let a man who has been passed over for promotion get an offer from another school and, unless there is a real wish to get rid of him, the offer will usually be met within limits (generally not equaled, just approached, for it is considered expensive to move, and the pattern is to offer new men more than those already in a department in order to induce them to transfer jobs) and the promotion will come through much more quickly than ordinarily.

Academic mobility is a large subject and, like any sociological phenomenon, is subject to a number of interlocking interpretations; some of the recent studies of academic life have devoted much effort to examining it in something of its complexity. But I think there is no question that, if we leave out entirely personal and private considerations (like those of health, for example, or a chance to do a particular kind of work, regardless of salary or status), academic mobility is most completely determined by the impulse for advancement. As G. B. Harrison put it in his book, *Profes-*

sion of English: "nor should the newcomer too rapidly put down deep roots. He will become the better teacher if he has achieved varied experiences of different kinds of university. In spite of the protests of his growing children, he gains in stature if he shifts his camp every ten years." I think Professor Harrison meant "rank and salary" by "stature"; gain in stature is incidental, although of course there is a kind of accrual of stature for the man who is known to have substantially improved his situation when he moves.

The ritual of "getting an offer" is intricate and formalized and must be carried through with utmost delicacy; it is not only a matter of the magic becoming ineffective if a slip is made: one can ritualize himself right out of a good job into a very poor one. When one feels slighted on a campus to the point where he is ready to make a change, he sounds around for possibilities, writing to former professors, to friends, reading the professional journals that carry announcements of jobs. It is better not to apply directly but to have someone else propose one's name, although it is not necessarily fatal to propose oneself with sufficient discretion. When an offer is made (after the usual negotiations of a visit to the campus, interviews, discussions of salary and teaching schedule, etc.), it is necessary to be ready to play one's hand to the limit before waving the letter or the telegram around. Bluffing is not simply dangerous; it is impossible: an administration always deals what cards it wishes. But an offer from an institution not lesser than one's own will often provoke prodigies of appreciation where nothing else will have any effect whatsoever.

The other-offer gambit can be worked only under limited conditions. It is not likely to be effective more than once in any rank, and it will not work at all at certain schools. Of course, at most of the schools where it will not work, one does not have to descend to such a maneuver to gain recognition, for the school will usually have bestowed it on its own. (At some schools, however, it does not work only because the chairmen and deans like nothing better than to involve themselves in the search for new personnel; it gives them a sense of power, and hiring new men is often a way of keeping the budget down.) An offer from a lesser school, or from a non-academic enterprise (a research laboratory, a publishing house, the government), is not considered an offer at all in the sense of providing any leverage. "You'll have to decide for yourself," a dean told a man who had been sounded out to join a research laboratory at double his professor's salary, "whether you want to stay in teaching or go into industry. We can't even begin to bid against private offers."

Where do all this side activity and all these carefully cultivated skills lead? Why, first to tenure, then to promotion, and, hopefully, sometimes, out of the classroom altogether. Rarely do they lead to authentic academic distinction. The most skilled practitioners of the academic art of how to succeed without actually doing anything (except cultivating the art of how to succeed without actually doing anything) are often persons with simple administrative ambitions. They do not want to teach, or to read, or to do research; they want to hire people and go to meetings and enjoy the perquisites of executive office. Which is always a shame, and sometimes can almost approach the tragic, for administration, properly viewed, is the most important activity on a campus. It makes a university what it is.

The plain fact is that advancement of genuinely worthy persons—who do indeed contribute valuably and discernibly by anyone's standards to the functioning and growth of a campus—is generally conceived of as being through administration. One can only feel ambivalent about this. The best administrators, the ones who know most intimately, most sensitively, most wisely, the meaning of administration are also likely to be the best teachers, the best researchers, the best faculty men in all ways. Those who are most needed in the classroom—or in the library or in the laboratory—are also those most needed in the offices of chairmen, deans, presidents.

Of course, on campuses which have a faculty of able men the way upward is rewarded with decent salary, decent teaching conditions, opportunities for continued work and growth, even various administrative responsibilities. It is only on poorer campuses that administrators are considered in the nature of clerks. And, for that matter, there is no reason at all for an administrator to forsake the classroom or the library forever. Some of the finest administrators insist on maintaining their activity as teachers and scholars; the roles of professor and administrator are by no means mutually exclusive.

Academic jokes often reveal how administration is regarded. One is about the madame of a brothel whom a regular client found working as just another girl in the establishment. When he expressed surprise, she shrugged. "Oh, I just got tired of administration," she explained.

"The president's job," goes one definition, "is to make speeches. The faculty's job is to think. The dean's job is to keep the president from thinking and the faculty from making speeches."

There is a gamut in the display of ambition from the poorest schools to the best, and sometimes this display can be used to define them. At poor schools, politicking in whatever appropriate ways present themselves is the most common way to achieve what is considered success on the local scene. At the best schools, productivity in one's discipline is the only way. The obverse also applies: politicking, espe-

197

cially of the cruder kind, of the sort that is entirely divested from productivity, is taboo at good institutions; productivity is often frowned upon, sometimes even discouraged or demeaned, at poorer schools (out of jealousy, incapacity to judge productivity). There is less opposition between a man's discipline orientation and his institution orientation at a good school, for these usually mingle there; a man's self-respect is part of his respect for the whole institution. While his disciplinary prestige might make him mobile, he is not likely to wish to move away if the institution's prestige depends in part at least on his own presence on the campus; his prestige, in turn, depends on the presence of his outstanding colleagues. At a poor institution, the men who are most comfortable and fulfill their ambitions most easily are those who seem oriented toward it alone, who project an aura of concern for this one place above all others, who sometimes even sneer at their own disciplines.

Of course, the prevalent situation on most campuses falls between the two extremes, between the campus overrun by petty politicians jockeying for position, and that dominated by outstanding academicians, so involved in their work that the running of affairs is sometimes neglected or left to lesser men. I don't suppose there is any ideal blending; one improvises. Discipline cannot be disregarded, nor can the daily operation of the plant. Perhaps a practical compromise is the one in which able professors move into administrative offices for periods and then out again, back to their disciplinary work. I am dubious about the effectiveness of mere professional administrators (former generals, former heads of corporations), except to raise funds or represent the campus before the legislature or the board of trustees, unless, of course, these professionals happen also to understand the nature of academic life in its intricacies and subtleties. A campus cannot be run like a brigade or a company or a government office.

If I am right in suggesting that academic man is in the aggregate, and particularly today, essentially modest, then it is not strange to find that ambition is suppressed, or turned to irrelevant ends, or even perverted to petty ones. If the security that comes with tenure (and with decent salary and minimally decent teaching conditions) is really the most important thing for professors, or at least for many of them, then we can understand that an ambition which drives one to anchor himself more firmly where he is necessarily cuts out an ambition which drives one upward. Perhaps this is one of the worst effects of the Depression, and one of the sorrier aspects of tenure. Mary McCarthy's president in *The Groves of Academe* ruminated about this: "I've fought all my life for better teaching conditions, more benefits, recognition of seniority along trade-union lines, and yet sometimes I wonder whether we're on the right track, whether as creative persons we shouldn't live with more daring. Can you have creative teaching side by side with this preoccupation with security, with the principle of regular promotion and recognition of seniority? God knows, in the big universities, this system has fostered a great many academic barnacles."

A fair question although, I think, one can answer yes. The concept of academic freedom and security has probably led to there being more academic giants than academic barnacles. Perhaps the freest university in the United States is also the greatest: Harvard (and those that approach it in stature—Columbia, Yale, Berkeley—are probably no less free). But I think President Hoar has at least a psychological point to make: the obsession with security has led to the drying up of ambition. Ambition involves running risks;

199

making bold ventures; encompassing wide possibilities. The academic world is not comfortable with ambition. The ambitious man is sneered at or feared. One is always assuming that the decent and outstanding man has no "ambitions." The chairman of a department at one of the great schools in the East was once asked whether he thought a colleague in another department, a man who had achieved an important reputation as a student in his discipline, a brilliant teacher, and a thoughtful observer of the American academic scene, might be interested in being considered for the presidency of a woman's college. The instinctive response the chairman gave was that he could not imagine that the professor would want to leave his students and his books, and so reported the response to the professor himself. "But, of course," the professor replied, "I should have liked to be considered for the job." And, indeed, what better place than as president of a college could a man with that professor's particular talents and concerns find for his energies and ambitions? Fortunately for everyone, the professor did become an important administrator at his own university.

But professors hesitate even to be ambitious in their own fields. As graduate students they are encouraged to develop the attitude that everything important has already been said, that they should not hope to make any significant contribution with their doctoral work, that they are best off "doing an edition" of someone obscure. You try to be modest and sure rather than immodest and unsure. Where once doctoral dissertations in English at Columbia, to cite only one place, could almost immediately be published and remain great works (Trilling's *Matthew Arnold,* Neff's *Carlyle and Mill,* Krutch's *Comedy and Conscience After the Restoration*), today students delimit their scope, they try to be safe and quick, and their work vanishes (except for the chapter or two that is transformed for publication in

200

a scholarly journal). If we read through the list of work in progress annually published in some discipline, we are confronted by a dreary anthology of all the dreary possibilities that dreary men can invent. It is astonishing that not one title should even promise to be of some importance. In the classroom, professors limit themselves to what has been said (whether it is good or bad is beside the point) by others on their subject; few men work with the substance of the course freshly, finding new perspectives, making venturesome generalizations.

In this atmosphere of academic staleness, it is no wonder that men with normal promptings of ambition, let alone with intenser ones, turn their energies into other channels away from the discipline to which they have committed themselves. Some become masters at obtaining fellowships and grants. Some embark on a career of a peripatetic rising through the ranks by using rungs at many different schools. Some devote themselves to campus politics, however degraded. Some all but go into business, most relevantly becoming roving consultants to private companies in their discipline, least relevantly, by investing in local real estate.

Ambition is not only a normal human drive, it is a healthy one, and no place less healthy, I think, than on a campus where able men dominate. It is ambition without talent, ambition that uses only itself, that becomes cynical and corrupt. Let campuses recognize clearly that there is enormous value for the world of the mind in the achievements which professors bring off, and ambition would not have to be hidden or masked. Let them recognize that ability is a positive quality, and administrators would not have to be looked on as academicians without ability for whom work had to be found. Surely, we shall always have to live with the decent hard-working, but little striving, little talented men in our midst. The quiet and smaller virtues are not to be demeaned or displaced, but they should not dominate campuses as though they were the prime virtues. Modesty, alas, is all too appropriately the right tone for most campuses today, for most have a great deal to be modest about, but confident and well-grounded boldness, of thought and of creation, is at least as appropriate as hesitant mediocrity. It is more appropriate for university life in general. There is nothing modest about Harvard, Columbia, Yale, Berkeley, Stanford, and nothing hollow either about the image they project. While we model ourselves in other, less important ways on these institutions, we do not try to emulate their upward thrust of speculation, assertion, achievement. Perhaps the only proper style is always to strive upward, but with content, along intellectually respectable lines, proud of our direction (not ashamed), indifferent to the jealous jeers from the sidelines, unafraid to ally ourselves with administrators (provided they are also in the movement), confident that this is the only natural and satisfying direction for all universities to take.

IN
LOCO PARENTIS:
CRAZY LIKE
A PARENT

In loco parentis, Elliot Cohen, late editor of *Commentary,* used to say, meant "crazy like a parent." He was characterizing the attitude of college administrations to their students. It may well be the most cogent summation of this attitude, for administrations, which often think of themselves more or less as acting in the place of parents, and sometimes say they are so acting, certainly behave as whimsically as any parent, or, rather, run the range of possibility of all parents, from being oversolicitous to being indifferent. There was a time when students were considered only a necessary nuisance. A famous story has a dean sighing to himself as he walks across a campus during a recess. "Isn't it wonderful, so peaceful and lovely," he says to an associate, "if we could only do away with students the year round." This is hyperbole, but like all hyperbole, it has a substance of truth. The ideal of many professors still is to have no students, to work at the Huntington or Folger libraries, or at the Rockefeller Institute or at the Institute for Advanced Studies (although some members of the Rockefeller Institute have recently gotten so lonesome for the classroom that the Institute has decided to offer advanced degrees to at least a few carefully selected, handsomely supported students).

Students always have nagged at faculty and administration by their very presence; they cannot ever be neglected. During my own undergraduate days, students were made to feel by most faculty that we were in their classes on sufferance. Some ten years later, when I returned to my alma mater, I discovered that the office of student affairs had begun to crawl with deans and assistant deans. Not that the college had suddenly begun to love students. The deans were appointed to create a buffer between students and faculty and higher administration; they were there, as one put it, "to solve the problem of students." I asked a dean a question about the nature of the student body. "Oh," she said, "that's not the sort of thing we're interested in although it's a good question. We just make statistical studies."

But administrations could not long continue pretending that students were just not there however many buffers they built. Their needs and their demands, even the development of their independent patterns of thought and behavior, forced institutions to take account of them, and not just by making mechanical gestures of interest. In addition, the growing self-consciousness within universities themselves, generated in part by their sheer expansion, by the quantitative increases producing changes in character, in part by the development of certain areas of sociology and psychology, also contributed to the university's awareness of students individually, as types, and as a whole society. Today institutions parallel parents in their unceasing concern about their charges. If no modern parent would think of raising a child without Spock and a smattering of Freud, no administration (or foundation) feels it can do right by students without Riesman, Eddy, Jacob, Sanford, and a host of other sociological and psychological experts. It is probably no exaggeration to say that "The American Student" has be-

204

come a separate area in the social sciences; he has come to constitute "a sub-culture."

The present moment may indeed be the fairest yet to assess the American student. The 'twenties, if we can judge from the literature of the time, was not a serious or happy period to be in college. Besides, too few enrolled. The 'thirties were marked by the Depression, and colleges, for those who could at least sustain themselves, were a refuge from the world of unemployment and menial jobs. The 'forties were given over to the war; the 'fifties were a time of intense adjustment to a partial peace. Today, there are few overriding preoccupations to displace legitimately a more or less full concern with one's work in college (obviously, I except such things as the atom bomb and the population "explosion"; but these are not of the immediately interfering order of wars or of depressions, at least not yet). Moreover, at no previous time have there been so many qualified students in college.

My own experience, which spans three decades, reveals the strikingly changed student landscape. I went to college in the late 'thirties and early 'forties, and started teaching in college, after a period in the Air Force, in the late 'forties, at the same time as I started work on my graduate degrees, which I got in the early 'fifties. Before the war, few persons without substantial means, for example, could think of entering graduate work except part-time, after completing other work. With the G.I. Bill, as well as the increased funds for all graduate education, it became possible for thousands upon thousands to go to graduate school as their main occupation. The principle of support of able students filtered down. Today, most private institutions turn away no qualified student simply because he has insufficient funds; scholarship money has increased enormously. (Even such once unattainable preparatory schools as Andover and

Exeter devote large sums to scholarships.) The City College of New York, a free institution, during the 'twenties, 'thirties, 'forties, and 'fifties, got the majority of able freshmen in New York. Today, it gets as a group, the second-best; most of the best get scholarships to private schools.

Fulbright, Smith-Mundt, and other funds have made foreign education a possibility for everyone at some stage. Previously, only the rich or the exceptional handful (Rhodes Scholars, for example) could think of Oxford or Cambridge or the Sorbonne. The present trend of going abroad, even for a short while, has widened emotional and intellectual horizons for all. Now the Grand Tour is not something just out of literature, something experienced by Byron and Shelley or by heroes and heroines of James novels; it is a reality for everyone ready and able to work towards it. Every campus has students who have been abroad, and every person on it, I venture, has been enriched as a consequence.

The world of the student has been affected in less discernible but perhaps more important ways as well. Many of the events and phenomena of this century that impinged on his total awareness, on his *weltanschauung* (which, of course, students have in a particularly intense form), also changed. The pressures on him of such things as the Spanish Civil War, the Depression, Hitler, Stalin, the draft, pressures which made their way into the classroom, which disrupted private life and private possibility, eased off. As prosperity slowly improved, the student's mobility increased. Especially with the G.I. Bill, but even without, he could go to schools away from home; he could buy second-hand cars; he could even, especially with parental subsidy, afford to fly to distant campuses.

All of the changes freed the student for a greater consciousness, of himself and of the world. He began to marry earlier, even as an undergraduate. In the 'thirties and 'forties, I never knew a married senior, let alone a married freshman. Today, my classes always have dozens of young married persons, husband and wife going to school at the same time. For good or bad, early marriage was simply not a practical possibility when I was a student. Fraternities and sororities are no longer the merely social centers they used to be; more and more serious students drop out of them altogether in their junior and senior years. While one may still make out good arguments for their utter abolition, these arguments could not with reason concentrate as heavily as they once did on the plainly pernicious effect these snobbish organizations can have on campus life. The Peace Corps seems to me a prime instance of the growth in maturity, in responsibility, in consciousness of the world, that marks the contemporary student in America. And when we have a football or basketball scandal on a campus, when some students at the University of Mississippi prove themselves to be barbaric hoodlums, we can cite other instances of civilized and honest behavior (the students at Clemson College, in South Carolina; the Freedom Riders, white and Negro) to keep the picture balanced.

Student interests seem to have changed fundamentally over the years: in the 'thirties and 'forties, these were focused on specific political situations (Spain, Germany; Communism); today, they are more likely to be generalized, dispersed, only rarely coming down to a particular problem at a particular time. The student demonstrations against the HUAC in the San Francisco area were not part of a nation-wide pattern. What did become a nation-wide concern, at least briefly, and still remains a concern here and there, is segregation, a more diffuse issue. Academic freedom for students, an important but somewhat vague concept, is another national concern. The National Student Association, while not neglecting political and social issues, seems most involved in an enterprise of self-identification, laying out patterns for definition of roles. My general impression is that students are today concerned, by and large, with remote philosophical questions rather than with immediate practical ones.

I have just come back from a student sponsored conference on my campus on the student's part in the university. It had some strange moments. The students wanted to be involved in such thorny administration and faculty functions as appointing or promoting professors, determining curriculum, defining the functions and objectives of a university. A number of professors and administrators present, conceding that students might well be consulted appropriately on all these matters, and were indeed already being consulted on some of them, were puzzled by the failure of the present student organization to solve smaller and more pressing problems. The campus newspaper for as long as anyone could remember had been operating in an atmosphere of crisis and uncertainty, generally understaffed, often attacked for not covering campus news adequately, or for slanting it. Seniors needing certain courses for graduation regularly find themselves locked out of these classes and have to wait a semester or even a year before they can graduate. The bookstore, ostensibly run by the students and subject to student council supervision, was always leaving students without textbooks essential in certain courses. Fraternities and sororities still discriminated against some minorities. None of these issues had been taken up adequately, let alone resolved. Yet the students wanted to be heard on the granting of tenure to faculty, on determining which courses students should take.

I am dubious about how much pressure should be exerted by students, a transient society, on faculty and administration, a continuous and permanent society. I say this aside

similar places, are certainly likely to be much better prepared for their college work than students at any state university, even one which can carefully choose its freshmen. But they are not likely to be superior to, say, a select group of honors freshmen at any particular half-way decent school, at least in potential.

This leveling in potential has meant that differences which develop later in attitude and achievement are likely to be accounted for more by the character of an institution than by that of its students. When students differ, as they do, it will be in manners, in regional attributes, in attitude toward learning, rather than in native intelligence. More than ever it seems important to distribute faculty talent widely so that no groups of students will be cheated. The similarity in values, drives, confusions, motivation of students falls within a discernible boundary, whether the students come from West or the East, from small private schools or large state ones. Of course, there will be differences in intensity of concern, in issues that agitate one group rather than another, in the originality with which attitudes are expressed. But, leaving aside such matters as a local demonstration against the House Un-American Activities Committee or discussions as to whether a Communist should be allowed to speak on a campus, it seems to me that students, when we can hear them through the organ music of generalization, have been asking the same thing everywhere. To oversimplify tremendously and to generalize shamelessly, I would say that students today want to have a greater part in shaping their education.

Riesman addresses himself to this issue, although he intimates that today's students lack the imagination and impulse to make their wishes effective, sometimes even to express them. Or, as Arthur Miller put it about students at his alma mater, the University of Michigan, they are

"afraid." "The relation of students to the curriculum," Riesman says, for example, "has a certain alienated quality, in
the sense that the students do not believe they have any
control over their own education." I think not. Nor do I
think that any paradox is involved, as Mr. Riesman suggests, in students wanting careers in large companies but
a modest and highly "conformist" family life. Students do
want to be involved in the large operation of running a
university, or at least to feel that they are involved, but
not to the extent of literally being responsible for policy
decisions. They will not have to live for long with the consequences of any real decisions, and they know it. They
want to be able to complain and to be attended to; they
want to make the institution and the world better places in
all ways; they want to feel that they are implicated in doing
something important. But they also do not want to over-
reach themselves. They want to be instructed, to be argued
out of extreme positions, to find the balanced and moderate
way. And their final effect is likely to be conservative rather
than radical.

No matter how we go at the question of students, we
must remember, as many of the studies point out, that few
will be on a campus—at least as students—for longer than
four years. Some few will remain as graduate students;
some simply as "professionals," forever attending classes.
But the majority come and go. The period they remain is
an important one, for them and for the country. But it
helps no one to think of them as a permanent citizenry.
Only the whole academic community is permanent, self-
perpetuating. And it is the welfare of this larger community
that should be the concern of everyone, students, professors,
administrators, the rest of the country. In our concern for
students, as in our concern for our children, we tend to neglect the larger area, the family, the entire society.

212

It is a favorite point to cite the experience of medieval students, who often chose their faculty and decided their curriculum. Surely the point might be used to prove how far we have gone in all areas—in university organization, in the concept of higher learning—in improving things. Which does not mean that we cannot still learn and borrow from earlier experiences in higher education. But we must not lose our sense of proportion, become ancestor worshippers, fetish treasurers.

It is a gross but easily made and understandable error to think of a campus simply as a microcosm, as a laboratory for students to practice or exercise political and intellectual skills. Grave confusions result. The slick campus politician may be misled into thinking he can readily transfer his skill to the larger world; the successful campus genius may take his local fame as a certain augury for the future. Lionel Trilling once neatly summed up this confusion: "It must be understood that there is no necessary correlation between undergraduate brilliance and actual intellectual accomplishment. It is not my impression that the most gifted of my students have done as well in the intellectual life as they gave me reason to expect, while some who have wearied me by their dullness or irritated me by their indifference have gone on to do admirable work. The circumstances in which the professional intellectual life is lived are very different from those of the classroom, and the qualities it needs are very different from those to which teachers usually respond."

At some point in the various studies of students, someone pauses to remark that, after all, students are why colleges and universities exist in the first place. Often this is said in the course of justifying a greater attention to student needs and wishes. I think no one on a campus would seriously deny the primacy of students. But to say this is not to say that students should, indeed, "run" affairs, or that anything should displace their only duty on a campus, to learn. All the studies of students' mental hygiene, value systems, political structures, ambitions, etc., etc., should be used in the interest of improving, if necessary, the student's performance *qua* student. His extra-curricular world should reinforce his classroom existence, not the classroom his activities in dormitory, union, or fraternity house. Students and some administrators are prone to forget that students, after all, are indeed on campuses as students, not as student leaders or editors or athletes or performers. To the extent that we become absorbed in the examination of students and their fascinating society, slighting their first identity, to that extent do we fail as faculty and administration.

One way of getting rid of students on a campus is to send them away on vacation. Another, and apparently more popular way, is to pretend that they are not really students at all but members of some strange and foreign culture. If we consider them anthropologically, we don't have to live with them or teach them.

WHO JUDGES
THE JUDGES?

ONE OF THE most frequently voiced complaints by students is about the grading system, a complaint they have been joined in by a number of prominent educators. Sometimes associated with the complaint about being constantly evaluated by their professors, is the wish to evaluate their professors. It is perhaps not as paradoxical as it seems at first for students, who complain about being judged, to want to judge their judges. In fact, one may well be considered the corollary of the other, for I sense that both come from an impulse to fuzz and blur some of the traditional character of contemporary American education. These two positions often cluster together with several others: disciplines should break down their sharp boundaries; we should have no examinations, or, at most, only final comprehensive ones; discussion should replace lecture.

David Riesman put the matter unequivocally. "Now, I am convinced," he once wrote, "that grades contaminate education—they are a kind of currency, which, like money, gets in the way of students' discovering their intellectual interests." And Oscar Handlin, also a professor at Harvard, in an article in *The Atlantic* entitled "Are the Colleges Killing Education?" put it with equal forcefulness. "The constant surveillance of their studies," he said about students, "serves no useful function and only interferes with their education." Both professors cite instances of how grades and examinations inhibit the educational process rather than aid it.

I confess that I am not only puzzled by the unmodulated way in which Professors Riesman and Handlin put their case, but also by their not seeming to see the issue in the largest possible context, that of all of the workings of a university.

Surely no one will argue that some courses, especially introductory ones but some advanced ones as well, have a fixed body of subject-matter, of concepts, of techniques of analysis, which must be learned before any student can go ahead in that field to do original work. How can a student of mathematics or physics or biology go through a sequence of courses, each of them dependent on the one before, without learning a certain amount of material in each one? A student of history, without some basic foundation in the facts and concepts of historical study? Some fields in their introductory courses leave little room for subjective and imaginative response. The substance of the course must simply be learned up to a minimal level before the student can go on to other things. And how can we determine how much the student learns except by examination, and how can we indicate the level of his attainment except by grades? (Some schools fudge the issues by pretending not to give "grades"; they do not stoop to A's, B's, or F's but grade by such appraisals as "satisfactory," "superior," "adequate," and the like. But these are grades just the same, whatever they are called.)

Obviously, many fields do not have a clear body of subject matter which must be learned; they develop skills in techniques and thought. English and perhaps philosophy

216

are such fields, although both also have divisions which call for the student to learn basic material (in English, the history of literature, including dates and contents of works; in philosophy, the history of philosophical thought, including dates and major works; both, of course, also require the student to understand and be able to evaluate the substantive matter of the history). In areas where subjective response is important and encouraged, grades obviously become more uncertain guides of achievement. Students with the gift of gab, or with a faster handwriting, or with a capacity to perform on tests, or with the talent to sense a professor's weakness or personal slant, will do better than equally prepared students without these side skills. In such subjects, as Handlin says, "only the reckless will dare not to know the right answers as the grader expects them, or allow questions to draw their thinking in unexpected directions."

But it is not the subjectivity and uncertainty of grades which so disturb Messrs. Riesman and Handlin; it is the grading system itself, however much it may be refined. It is the competitiveness implicit in the "currency" value of grades that is deplored. Of course, every instructor can cite case after case of the "greasy grind," out to make grades at any cost, including, if necessary, dispensing with actual learning. I can remember classmates of mine who spent much of their time figuring out which professors to take to keep up their grade averages, and then, if they made a mistake, a great deal more time, figuring how to beat the professor at his game. For all they might have learned in such pursuits, this was a learning entirely irrelevant to college. With equal effort, they could just as easily have gotten the material of the course. And we all know students, perfectly able young men and women, cast into despair by not achieving the grades they wanted or deserved.

But I do not see what any of this proves except that an inordinate value has been put on grades; it does not mean that the grading system is in itself wrong. Riesman cites a study at the University of Chicago of the success of students. It was "concluded," he writes, "that those students frequently fared best who were not too obedient, who did not get an undiluted, uncomplicated, straight-A record. (The straight-A students, in fact, sometimes slipped away without anyone's noticing.)" Precisely: sensible academic persons know how to evaluate grades properly. They are only one of several estimates made of a student's potential.

Handlin remarks that "every teacher has seen the slow starter work at his own pace, then suddenly discover himself and out-distance the front-runners." Again: precisely. *Every teacher* of sense and experience makes allowances for all sorts of individual variation: slow starting; incapacity to take objective examinations; over-capacity for taking certain kinds of examination; brilliance that leaps beyond any anticipation; erratic originality that works elliptically and privately and, sometimes, incomprehensibly; steadiness that in itself attains a high level of ordering and understanding. And every teacher of sense and experience takes all such matters into account when evaluating a student, whether by grades or in writing a confidential estimate.

I have been intimately involved in an honors program for the past seven years. About fifteen students meet in a colloquium once a week for two hours with two professors. We all read a book a week, and the students write papers on the books to start the discussion; the papers are intended to help them crystalize their reaction. One semester, we thought that we would not grade the papers, but simply write comments on them. After all, there is no right and wrong in this sort of thing. The students asked after a while to be given grades so that they would have some notion of how relevantly, how cogently, they were reading the books. (These grades sometimes bore only a remote relation to the final one, for the final grade was based on class discussion, and on the highest rather than on the average performance, and was considered as much an estimate of the student's future success in honors as of his current work.) The point is that these students themselves, allowed and encouraged to range freely, felt that the grades gave them one quick measurement. And that's all college grades can ever do.

College proceeds by intervals, by steps of achievement. There can be no other way unless we are ready to advocate a four-year bull session, starting anywhere and ending anywhere, which I know some observers are in favor of. But if we are not ready to go to the peripatetic, free floating, unstructured arrangement advocated so eloquently by Paul Goodman, we must recognize that the dynamics of college require grades. They help the students themselves make the ascent from one level to another. Grades will always be crude, reductive measures of students, but if they are recognized as such, as I think they are, some of their worst effects will be minimized. Not even Phi Beta Kappa asks for a straight-A average (although its practice of selecting a certain portion of the top members of a class encourages competitiveness). And the very dubious status of Phi Beta Kappa key holders today testifies to the reservations with which grades are widely regarded.

What is needed on the subject of grades, as elsewhere, is a rigorous and open investigation of their significance. The fools in the faculty and in the student body, if they cannot learn through experience the limited meaning of grades, should have some of the point made for them explicitly, if any such even moderately subtle point can penetrate their sometimes willful density. In a sensible environment, grades are used sensibly.

Perhaps equally urgent is a wider recognition that, as Handlin puts it, "not all learning in the college community of the past was confined to the classroom. Often the students taught each other more effectively than the teachers could, gained more from extracurricular activities than from formal classwork." Of course, but we cannot pretend that the classroom with all of its exigencies is really being replaced, or that we can hope to know in any practical way, for the purposes of helping a student move properly through college, just what value extra-curricular activities actually have. That value is the student's private choice and affair; it is supplementary to that of the classroom: otherwise, why bother with class at all? Why not, as indeed some students (and some faculty too) do, simply specialize in extra-curricular affairs? I do not share Professor Handlin's concern that "there will be ever less time for [students to participate in extra-curricular affairs] as the shadow of the examination falls across the college. Boys made rivals by competition will be less ready to help one another, and the immensely variegated activities of the college as it was may dry up." Campus life outside the classroom, for one thing, is likely to be far more competitive and demanding, and less fairly so, than in the classroom; for another, it is the classroom that has to fear the student union, not the union the classroom.

With students, the objection to grades has often seemed to me an objection to discipline of any sort. Why should they have to know a fixed body of material? Why, if they want to be literary critics, should they have to read, say, Dryden's criticism, or that of Wordsworth and Coleridge? Can't they work on Faulkner or Hemingway without going through all the nonsense of the past? Why can't they be original in philosophy, sociology, history, government classes? Haven't they eyes and ears, haven't they seen and heard enough to talk about anything? Why must they be subjected to endless scrutiny? They've done their reading and their thinking; why can't professors believe them? Why the constant challenge, the demand for proof, the endless measuring? Why do they have to do just what everyone else is told? Doesn't originality count as well as conformity and neatness?

These all seem like plausible challenges, and sometimes they are honest and reasonable as well. I have had students who have asked whether they might not try writing sonnets in an English class rather than doing the more conventional assignments. They have turned in interesting efforts, revealing clearly that they have wrestled with the form and have learned to understand something of the energy and labor that goes into creative work. But others have told me that they are writing a novel "in their heads," and that the work will be great. Some have developed the high art of student gamesmanship to dupe the most skeptical instructor. One bohemian type, who talked and gestured a remarkably impressive game of intimacy with modern poetry, impressing her fellows and some professors, turned out—when she was finally cornered into taking an examination, consisting of both objective and essay questions—to be both ignorant and illiterate—although not stupid.

Students often tend to rate their instructors, I think unconsciously, on how well they can con them. The instructor who can be carried away by student enthusiasms is considered "responsive" to student needs and capacities. A favorite ploy of the *luft*-student, the student who lives on air, is to divert class discussion into intriguing side roads. The instructor who generally goes along on these excursions, responding to student "interest," is much admired, especially if his examinations then proceed to examine the side issues, or if he gives no examinations, or if he gives all students high grades for "class participation."

Not all students, of course, who wish to be involved in faculty evaluation are of this sort. Many outstanding students, indeed, feel that some of their professors simply are incompetent, and they are quite likely to know this better than colleagues or administrators. But the impulse toward asking for student participation in tenure or promotion decisions of faculty comes, I think, from a fundamental wish to make over the character of college education in the direction of the continuous bull session. In part, I say this because those instances I have seen of students pressuring to have their opinions on faculty performance given heed have involved professors who have been grand discussion leaders but who, sometimes by their own admission, did not bother to cover a subject matter, or, more importantly, to be active in their chosen field, keeping up with current work, as evidenced by publication or other sorts of productivity. In larger part, however, I say this because of the philosophical and practical implications of student evaluation of faculty.

Some work has been done to show that student evaluation can be carried out effectively and meaningfully, and I am ready to stipulate that our advances in the area of all such measurements of opinion and appraisal have been so considerable that a proper evaluation would indeed reveal something of a professor's competence in the classroom. But how would such an evaluation be used? I have known professors who have used self-evaluation measures (some of them very crude ones, it is true, and some administered before final grades were assigned) simply to broadcast how high they rated; such persons had no other claim to advancement. Any system of showing evaluations only to the professors, for their own private benefit, breaks down as soon as one professor starts publicizing good results. This would be like a secret ballot in a small group in which the participants start announcing their votes; there's no way of checking, and others, more reticent, have their privacy violated.

Should an administration use such evaluation even in part to advance or to hold back a man? (I am assuming that all sorts of halo effects—the upgrading of a professor who gives high marks; the downgrading of one who gives low; etc.—have been effectively eliminated or controlled). I think not. The value of a student estimate of a professor implies that a student can truly know how good a professor is. This seems to me a dubious proposition, at least at this stage in our knowledge of the classroom process. No matter how impeccable and extensive any measurement, it cannot tell how deeply a professor has penetrated into a student's consciousness. If, as Handlin says, we cannot say how much students learn *outside* the classroom, how can we tell how much he learns *inside* the classroom? The student may think he has learned so much; the professor may even think he knows, roughly, how much each student has learned. But learning does not stop with the final examination. It may go on for years. An attitude of mind may be instilled which will not reach full fruition until the student has gone into the world and been there for a good period. I still respond, sometimes with a start, to things which first implanted themselves in undergraduate, let alone graduate classes. I think I may be closer now to estimating truly the effectiveness of some of my teachers, but, precisely because I am still learning from them (sometimes even negatively, as I reject some of their teaching), I would hesitate to fix an evaluation.

Now, I am not dismissing the usefulness of student evaluation, if these are devised so as to be more than popularity

223

contests, and if they are not used by administrators as the sole criterion for a total evaluation. (I have heard of one college president who threw away all other considerations in granting tenure or salary increases or promotion, and relied entirely on a ballot of professor popularity conducted by the fraternities and sororities.) But a fair and "safe" evaluating tool, judiciously applied, may finally not offer much more evidence than is already available and may simply be too costly, in time and money, to be worth the effort. I think there are few campuses where everyone does not know who are the best and the worst teachers. And within our present system of electives and multiple section courses, students indicate their sense of good and bad teaching, a sense not wholly determined by grades or entertainment alone. (Of course, it is important for natural selection to operate that a required course, wherever possible, not be taught as a monopoly by only one person.)

Time and again the suggestion is made that the traditional curriculum ought to be revised. It is said that division of English and history courses into chronological periods or into types, or of sociology and philosophy courses into discrete areas, or of mathematics and physics into a fixed sequence, fragments learning into artificial little units, de-emphasizes the interconnectedness of a discipline, and of one discipline with another, and leads to a compartmentalization that stresses specialization to the detriment of over-all comprehension. It is true that a professor teaching the 17th century in English literature may well not be as intimately informed about the 18th as he should be, and that the specialist in European medieval history may be hazy about contemporary Latin American history. It is true that it is important for student and teacher in any field to have an over-all sense of his subject. But I am not sure that what follows is that we should jumble all our courses together.

My impression is that student and faculty "generalists" usually do not want to root themselves anywhere. They prefer to "specialize" in "things in general." Although they argue that the person who works in a larger area understands and knows more than the one who absorbs only a small one, the fact is that it is sometimes easier to talk about all history than about the history of a particular country at a particular time. The "appreciation" of history, like that of science, or of literature, or of art, is much easier to teach and to learn than is 18th century French history, or zoology, or the drama of the Restoration, or the techniques and theories of post-Impressionist painters. It is important to have large integrating courses that cut across all areas, that provide a large perspective, but only as a supplement to the traditional curriculum (which, of course, should always be subject to revision as new arrangements suggest themselves). A college devoted to things in general is finally devoted to nothing at all.

Associated with an objection to grades and the traditional curriculum is an objection to examinations. Students and faculty feel superior to the housekeeping drudgery of tests. Handlin puts this association neatly. "I tease myself sometimes," he writes, "with daydreams of how we might break out of the present situation. A few institutions have already separated the teaching and marking functions. That is as it should be, and the result is to clarify the relationship of the teacher to his students. It would be gratifying to appear in a classroom where everyone was on the same side, where there was not one to police and the others to be policed, but all were to work toward the same end. Evidence points to the merits of a divorce between the essentially incompatible tasks of instructor and grader. . . . No other system

225

of higher education subjects its students to the endlessly badgering tests of the American college. The examinations of French and English universities are difficult, but they come where they belong, at the terminus of a stage in education. And they probe not fragments of courses, but the mastery of a whole field of knowledge, however and whenever acquired."

If Handlin really believes that examinations are *only* a form of policing, it seems to me that he altogether misconceives the intent and use of examinations. Examinations are one of the simplest ways for students to make order out of their learning; they are one of the simplest ways for an instructor to relate the learning in his classroom to his teaching. They are essential, I submit, to the teaching-learning dialogue. Students need to pause and to sort out, systematize, arrange, absorb what has been going on, not only in the classroom, but in the library and in their own discussions; frequently serious students want examinations to help them in their learning. Now, of course, examinations on different levels will have to differ as to purpose; in freshman English courses, for example, examinations may well be a form of policing, usually just to see that the brainwashing of high school misinformation is effective. But on higher levels, examinations have nothing to do with policing at all. For example, in junior, senior, and graduate courses, examinations are simply another teaching and learning aid. Too many tests are certainly a nuisance to teacher and student, but none at all will work all sorts of questionable pedagogic results: students will not keep up with the continuing work of the class, leaving it for the last minute; some few students, even when they keep up, will not really understand the work; the class will tend to descend (or ascend, I suppose) to vague discussions around the material of the course instead of engaging with the

226

material itself. I would be delighted to have someone else mark my students, and, indeed, in introductory courses assistants have become widely available. In advanced work, however, it seems to me essential for an instructor, especially if he has larger classes, or if he lectures more than he conducts discussion, to have examinations as a way of determining how well he is communicating. Otherwise he may simply be talking to himself.

The French and English systems Handlin cites, also practiced in some places in this country (the graduate English department at Columbia, for example), have their own pitfalls. Some French and English students, particularly those who have gone through a disciplined and rigorous tutorial system beforehand, certainly produce meaningful results on such examinations. But many, skilled in testmanship and other forms of gamesmanship, use the European system merely to attain a gloss of learning, a veneer that becomes transparent when they have to deal with substance. I have known both sorts of European scholars, and the latter, while not common, suggests that the system is not without its defects. A European mathematician once confided that the system indeed encourages frauds. In the American system, someone who skims the surface of his discipline, learning to drop names of books, learning to indicate by a shrug or the raising of an eyebrow an intimacy with his subject matter that it would be vulgar to challenge, will come a cropper long before graduation if he has to take examinations along the way. At Columbia, the oral examination in English was a terrifying ordeal, traumatic and disturbing to many students, and not always the best measurement of a student's learning. No doubt the system spared the professors from the regular and tedious chore of reading periodic examinations, leaving them free to do other work, but fakers got through, the timid dropped out of school altogether (and timidity is not a reliable counter-indication for college teaching), and the experience left every candidate in some state of shock. (I must confess that, all in all, I would not change the Columbia system but simply suggest that the examination be made less catastrophic, less like the final day of judgment; I understand that improvement has taken place in recent years.)

The challenge to grading, the theory that students ought to evaluate faculty, the wish to replace the present subject and area oriented curriculum, the objection to examinations, seem to me to have at their source a misconception of the student role in college. The misconception is by no means limited to students; indeed, it may have been voiced first by professors, and it is certainly encouraged by many professors and some administrations. It has to do with conceiving of college as a world in which students are supposed *primarily* to grow up. Any learning they do is thought of as incidental, sometimes indeed (especially when examinations and grading systems are objected to) as interfering with the maturing process. Many professors when asked what they think their function is answer that it is to help students learn to think and to grow up. Few are so "old-fashioned"—or so daring—as to say "to teach" and to see that the students learn. Students, when justifying a frenetic, time and energy consuming extra-curricular life, explain that they are learning to live with the problems of the real world.

No question that life adjustment, growing up, are important processes, and, for college students, they obviously must take place on a campus. Every professor, administrator, and student should realize this. But these are extra-classroom problems, they are complementary but subordinate to the classroom process. Too many teachers take their role as surrogate parent too intensely, with sometimes un-

228

comfortable and unhappy consequences. The teacher who is always conferring with and advising students, helping them "grow up," will not only be neglecting his first responsibility as a teacher and scholar, but will also probably not be helping the student much, for he is likely to be an amateur at any sort of counseling. Of course, on campuses without a guidance service—psychiatrists, psychologists, social workers—professors will often have to do double duty, and on any campus, there will be professors with whom students have an especially sensitive rapport. Professors—like students—are human, and situations will always arise, naturally and wholesomely, in which one person tries to help another.

But the question is one of emphasis, of orientation. Some studies of student societies make the campus seem like one huge group therapy laboratory. Classrooms are smaller units to practice group dynamics (or group therapy). Conferences are like psychoanalytic sessions. Students have to be patted on the head, held by the hand, bottle-fed (some of the campuses specializing in this big brother relationship have nearby bars, where afternoon beer sessions are popular places for carrying on this uplifting group work). And I would say that to the extent that any of this activity, however excessive and seemingly irrelevant, contributes to an intensification of genuine intellectual activity, it is justified. Much of it, of course, not only does not contribute; it interferes.

The boom in student sociology comes from outside the classroom, from personnel deans, from administrators. As I indicated earlier, it was a natural enough development as student society increased in numbers, as self-appraisal became necessary for universities growing and meeting new needs. And I think there is no doubt that when professors become aware of the buzzing, booming, swirling world of students, they cannot but be affected in their teaching. Too few professors, of course, do become aware of their students as persons; in fact, too few become aware of any of the huge amount of research done right under their noses about students. More should certainly know of the separate society that surrounds them.

But the student sociologists should not distort the landscape which they are examining. The culture they study has more than one center of activity; the only reason that students are on campus in the first place is to go to class. It is the classroom which defines a student. (I use classroom in the wide sense, to include any teaching-learning situation.) A student without a classroom has no identity as a student.

THE
FUTURE
LANDSCAPE

IF ANYONE had tried to predict, in
the late 'forties, after World War II ended, what the academic landscape would look like in twenty to twenty-five years, I think he would have missed some of the most important transformations. Higher education had to recover from the period of lethargy imposed by war; it had to recover its inherently dynamic nature. Today one might quite accurately predict what will happen in the next twenty to twenty-five years, not that we have any blueprints before us, but because so many of the forces gaining momentum have already become clear.

We can expect to see a whole new institutional arrangement arising. The pattern of the Associated Colleges at Claremont has proved itself more than workable; it has proved that a cluster of small colleges, pooling resources, concentrating on separate kinds of undergraduate and on a select graduate education, can offer to students and faculty more than isolated small colleges can. Already under way are plans to consolidate groups of independent institutions into a loose federation, in New England, in the Great Lakes region. The state university system in California will include as one of its units a campus of independent colleges. In the Mid-west, several universities have agreed to allow students to take courses at other campuses for full credit on their own campus. That redistribution of our academic wealth which would seem so desirable has begun in the form of small, sometimes hesitant gestures, which suggest that the principle has been accepted in theory.

Within institutions we will find all sorts of changes and modifications in tradition. Whether or not academic plants will expand to house the vast numbers of students, adjustments will be made. The conventional four-year period to attain a baccalaureate will undoubtedly be decreased, one way or another. As professional training builds more and more on a foundation of undergraduate education, the pressures to reduce the time in undergraduate work without skimping on content and quality will force the curriculum to go to three years, or fewer. The University of Pittsburgh has gone on an all-year basis to allow this reduction. Antioch College now includes a summer session, equal in length to the other quarters, as a regular part of the academic year; students may even enter during the summer, immediately on graduation from high school. In addition to going on a regularized full-year basis of operation (most schools now have truncated summer sessions, which only pretend to be equal to the regular ones), schools will probably be using facilities for more hours during the day. The library at the State University of Iowa has long been open 24 hours daily.

We will probably see the wider adoption of effective mechanical aids, educational television in certain subjects, films, tapes, teaching machines. A class of master teachers, senior professors, will probably emerge, concentrating on the essence of their field, leaving introduction to beginning teachers, or, in some few cases (mathematics drill, English drill), even to machines. Already there is a professorial elite in engineering and the physical sciences, with professors earning salaries in the twenty thousands all over the country, which put them in the company of the managerial elite, sometimes literally, as they are asked to sit on boards of large companies, to advise on the future. But it seems to me inevitable that professors in all other disciplines as well will eventually rise in status; indeed, it is not inconceivable that the professor in a narrow, rare, and "useless" field will become even more sought after as the ranks of the engineers, physicists, chemists swell in response to the emphasis put on their disciplines today.

As the status of professors increases, it is likely that their academic freedom and security will increase. Here, paradoxically, the work of the AAUP, so heavily concentrated on improving professional working conditions of faculty, will scarcely be needed any longer; the free market, I think, will accomplish relatively quickly and effectively what the AAUP has for so long been straining to achieve. As professors attain a greater mobility and independence, the concept of tenure will probably lose some of its practical force. The dignity of the profession will necessarily improve in the whole society. The New Deal in the 'thirties was perhaps premature in using so many academic persons in government; the New Frontier uses even more and with much less public distress. "Professor" will slowly lose any ironic import; doctors of philosophy will stop trying to hide their designation under the guise of modesty by calling themselves "mister." Not that the AAUP will waste away, but its concerns and the thrust of its philosophy will have to be considerably modified. It will perhaps be able to concern itself with more "universal" and "philosophical" issues, establishing a code of ethics, say, or devoting itself to considering what many think an insoluble problem: the definition of professorial competence. It may well become much more like the American Bar Association than a trade union, with which it has been pejoratively but not altogether inaccurately compared.

The internal structure of universities will likely become much more flexible, with departments flowing into departments, and with some departments eventually disappearing. Separate new areas of study will emerge; we can already see the beginnings of some: bio-physics; interdisciplinary studies; new applications of psychology. As entering college students become more literate, not just in English but in foreign languages too, departments of literature will change their emphasis, or perhaps even their nature. If a separate class of professional administrators does not develop, trained in the intricacies of running a university, leaving professors to their primary work, as such a class has developed in medicine, to run hospitals for example, then we might expect a greater integration of teaching with administration, with a freer exchange between laboratory and classroom on the one hand and the deans' and chairmen's offices on the other.

The Ph.D. degree will be revitalized, the master's degree will begin to have more meaning, or be eliminated altogether, the bachelor's will indicate both a more meaningfully ranging liberal education as well as a fuller preparation for graduate work. As higher education sloughs off fat and idle piddling, concentrating on muscle and fruitful work, the high schools and the elementary schools will necessarily have to strengthen curriculum, stiffen standards. Of course, it is entirely possible that a parallel system of lowest to highest education will establish itself, devoted to a full-fledged carrying out of some of the more extreme educationist notions, which hold not only that every American child is entitled to an education but also to a real, honest-to-goodness college degree. Signs of this are apparent in the twin systems of higher education in California, and in the presence in nearly every state of a "good" school, part of the mainstream of American education, and a former school of agriculture, now called university, which is an "easier" one, which gives the same degrees as the "good" schools but usually to persons unable to get them there. (It is inaccurate to generalize about which school is "good" and which "easy," for in some states the former aggie college is the dominant and good one, and the traditional university has simply gone off the main track.)

I think that the vast gap separating the Harvards and Yales from the state universities will be narrowing. Already the gap has narrowed between Harvard and Yale and such state universities as those in California, Illinois, Indiana, most evidently on the graduate level. With an ever increasing support of higher education everywhere, from foundations, from state legislatures, from Washington, from large companies, from individual philanthropists, it is likely that the gaps will become very small ones indeed, perhaps nonexistent as universities begin to share resources.

The character of student work will have to change dramatically. The social aspect of undergraduate schools will disappear very nearly completely; sororities and fraternities will become housing centers mainly, as they have done on some campuses. The private universities are steadily raising standards for admission, as are public ones, and serious undergraduate life will no longer have room for the Joe and Jane Colleges, who still clutter up classrooms while looking for mates or forestalling the day they will have to make an honest living. Students at any self-respecting school will have to work nearly full time, close to year-round, to complete the intensified, expanded, and concentrated curriculum. Creative work in painting, writing, music, drama will center more and more on campuses. It is likely that dental, medical, and law schools, which are still largely post-graduate professional schools, will reach down into the early years of college and integrate professional and liberal education.

Perhaps the most striking change in the character of students will come with the growth of what is today called variously "adult" or "continuing" education. High school students who did not go to college for one reason or another will find themselves registering for degree work, sometimes out of necessity, to meet increasing demands for college-trained personnel, sometimes out of plain personal desire, the result of a matured attitude toward education. College students who drop out before completing their work will also be returning in increased numbers. As the working week throughout the country continues to become shorter, we may expect to see unions and companies encouraging attendance in college; already some unions and companies have begun subsidizing college students.

In addition to the older students coming to college for the first time, or to complete work for degrees, many college graduates whose lives have taken them far afield from the concerns and attitudes of the academic world, will be wishing to return for "extension" work, courses or lectures offering no credit but only the opportunity to read and learn. Such "community" courses are well established all over the country now, of course, but we may expect them to spread, expand their coverage, increase their number, as leisure becomes more available, or perhaps simply as the fashion to be intellectually alert catches on.

It is likely, too, that students will become, as McGeorge Bundy puts it, "partners" in the enterprise of higher education. Graduate students, of course, have long functioned as colleagues, teaching or supervising introductory courses, pursuing research. Undergraduates will surely begin to take over some of these duties also. Already, the Ford Foundation Three Year Master's Program calls for students to begin their apprenticeship for college teaching in their

236

junior and senior years. At the University of New Mexico, senior honors students have replaced one member of the two-men faculty team for some of the freshman honors colloquia. Many college students in education begin their high school teaching, under close supervision of course, in their last year of college; theoretically, there is no reason why college seniors should not be able to instruct freshmen in their discipline, especially under proper supervision and in introductory material that is part of their own work. Also, as student quality keeps improving, that is, as their preparation becomes more thorough and intensive, more and more students will be taking their place alongside their professors, as associates rather than as mere disciples, in some fields actually functioning as members of a unit of which the professor will only be the leader.

McGeorge Bundy has covered many of these points in his summation of the features of an academic utopia, which he envisions as coming in 1975. He pretends to be speaking in that year. "The first and in many ways the greatest of our accomplishments," he says, "has been to rub out most of the distinctions separating the student, the teacher, and the research scholar." He declares that the distinction between administrator and professor has also "faded away," that the dividing line "between membership and nonmembership in the university community itself" has disappeared, that "it is no longer queer for seniors to help in the learning of freshmen," and, most importantly, that the academy has learned to accept "change itself as a necessary part of existence."

Some of the changes we may expect in the future will certainly take place whether we like them or not, and whether they are good or bad. It is inevitable that the pressure of numbers, the pressures of a changing society and of a changing world, will work their will whatever resistance is put up. But I think that it will always remain possible to preserve a sense of the past however turbulent the present, that permanent values can be made to survive and flourish in the midst of transient ones. At every moment, the idea of a university must be kept in mind and kept alive.

Here I think the prospect is most hopeful. Several of the larger, wealthier, and more heavily populated states have devoted much intelligent thought to developing "master plans" so that disorder and chaos will not result. California is planning new small colleges, the enlargement of existing institutions, and the creation of new large campuses. Other states have similar plans. Within any state university, committed by its nature to grow as its population grows, honors programs may be established, to bring to qualified students the intensive work and close attention, the intellectual intimacy among students and professors, that mark small Ivy League colleges. The creation of small colleges within existing large colleges is one ready way to fight the destructiveness that can come with immensity.

The tradition of individual scholarship seems to be in no jeopardy. The hysterical alarmists who imagine all professors reduced to shouting through megaphones or booming through microphones to thousands of students will surely not prove right. Foundation and institution support of library and laboratory research, while leaving many things to be desired and to be corrected, has been steadily and imaginatively expanding. Mechanical aids of various sorts can only in the long run help the professor, not sabotage or replace him. The university is bound to become more nearly what those of us in it have always wanted it to be, in Bundy's words: "a home, for hours, or days, or weeks at a time, of all highly civilized men."

So much, then, we can tell about the future from the signs in the present.

For all of the hopeful and clear signs for the future, some

things are still not plain, and it would be a mistake, I think, to suppose that all necessary progress will be made in any natural course of events without active and highly conscious control. It is essential at every minute to keep aware of main streams and side streams, and to know, at least, the general direction of any particular current, and to know whether we are moving or not, and why. We may want to divert or even to reverse some of the plain tendencies. Perhaps the most hopeful sign for the future is simply that the territory of higher education has been so fully opened for scrutiny.

The time seems peculiarly right now to enter the academic landscape and begin an examination of it from the inside out. Too many studies have circled over a particular locale, viewing it thoroughly and carefully no doubt, but from a height. The studies of some of the more piquant sectors of faculty society—*The Academic Marketplace, The Academic Mind*—have provided a full and rich background which we can now begin to take for granted and put to use for studies that get down to earth, that get into individual departments, laboratories, classrooms. What makes a good teacher? What makes good teaching? Is effective teaching possible without a good teacher? How do students learn? What makes a teacher good or better, or bad and worse? Projects have been under way for some while to study the Russian character through Russian literature. In the course of its probing, it is hoped that some group (or individual) will devote at least some systematic effort to an unsparing examination of the academic character through the fiction and essays written about it. Surely novels and memoirs and essayistic appraisals (like Barzun's *Teacher in America*) will not replace more conventional sociological analysis in helping us know some of the phenomena that operate in the more obscure but nevertheless significant corners of the

239

landscape, but they might well, in cumulative effect, offer much understanding, and they may well point to particular kinds of controlled probing that might profitably take place.

Indeed, the burgeoning interest in academic study—that library of books, pamphlets, and surveys on students, for example—may suggest that we are in a process of insulating ourselves from the inner landscape, which is a difficult and delicate one to enter. But it is that innermost landscape which is our ultimate concern. How teaching and learning take place, what should be taught and how it should be learned (facts? techniques? ideas? concepts? to be remembered for the next test? to be absorbed for a lifetime? to change or deepen attitudes? to prepare for living? or for working? and for what kind of world?), are of the essence. All of the mighty and varied apparatus established and being established to study higher education—the changing U.S. Office of Education; the association of graduate schools; the founding of centers to study higher education, like the one at Berkeley; the whole new area of academic sociology—will eventually have to get around to considering the fundamental issues. It may be, of course, that the huge mountains of work being done on peripheral geography are all preparatory to moving in on the central territory, and if so we can take heart that the approaches are being built so substantially, but it may also be that all of this impressive effort is a way of avoiding getting to the inner territory. The mountains may, indeed, be blocking it off from sight.

My sense remains optimistic. Professors and students have the occupational affliction of articulateness. So long as they will speak out, and it is impossible to imagine any widespread dulling of the responsive and analytic instincts even under the pressures of the present upheavals, our first concerns will not long be neglected. It is impossible to imagine an academic complacency blighting the present and future landscape. The point is to put alertness and imaginative concern to proper use, not to adapt it to still another fringe study of the workings of the academic person, student or faculty. The voices from within have at least as much to say as those outside and distant. With all the vigorous attention being paid to the landscape, I cannot conceive that these voices will not be heard and not be attended to. It is perhaps not accurate to speak of any golden "age" of universities in Western culture although there have been periods of greatness of individual universities, and for a particular time, a group of universities may have indeed ascended so high above their surroundings that the "age" indeed seemed great. We will always be limited by the availability of rich human resources; there are only so many great professors, so many outstanding students, and the most determinedly organized arrangements to establish and find greatness will not do very much to increase the natural supply. Yet I think, given the truly immense and serious concern about the future beginning to dominate the academic landscape everywhere, that only a concerted effort to keep from fulfillment (for some philosophical reason: it would be "undemocratic"; or some widespread limitation of mind, which is implausible) can prevent American academic life from attaining a hitherto unapproached level of true greatness.